Stockholm in 3 days

Welcome to Stockholm, the vibrant and picturesque capital of Sweden! This city is renowned for its stunning architecture, rich cultural heritage, and beautiful natural surroundings. Located on the east coast of Sweden, Stockholm is situated on 14 islands, making it a unique and dynamic destination.

Stockholm is a city with a fascinating history, which can be seen in its many museums, historic buildings, and landmarks. It is also a city that is constantly evolving, with a thriving art scene, innovative cuisine, and vibrant nightlife.

When it comes to exploring Stockholm, there is plenty to see and do. From strolling through the charming cobblestone streets of Gamla Stan, the old town, to visiting world-renowned museums such as the Vasa Museum and Skansen Open-Air Museum, there is something for everyone in Stockholm.

This guide will provide you with all the information you need to make the most of your visit to Stockholm. We'll cover the best attractions, activities, and cultural experiences that Stockholm has to offer, as well as practical tips for getting around the city and staying safe. Whether you're interested in history, art, nature, or just soaking up the local culture, Stockholm is sure to captivate and inspire you. So let's dive in and explore this beautiful city together!

Table of Contents

Stockholm in 3 days - Travel Guide..1
1. Introduction 5
    1.1 The History of Stockholm 7
    1.2 Stockholm's Geography and Climate 9
    1.3. Swedish Language and Culture..9
    1.4 10 Must-Know Swedish Personalities from History 11
    1.5 Top Attractions in Stockholm..13
    1.6 When to Visit Stockholm 17
    1.7 FAQs: travelling to Stockholm..19
2. Getting To Stockholm 21
    2.1. Flights and Airports 23
    2.2. Train and Bus Connections 24
    2.3. Cruise and Ferry Services 24
    2.4. Visa Requirements and Entry Regulations 25
3. Getting Around Stockholm 27
    3.1. Public Transportation 28
    3.1.1. Subway (Tunnelbana) 28
    3.1.2. Buses and Trams 28
    3.1.3. Commuter Trains (Pendeltåg) 30
    3.2. Biking in Stockholm 30
    3.3. Taxis and Ridesharing Services....................................30
    3.4. Car Rentals and Driving 31
    3.5. Walking and Accessibility 31
4. Where to stay in Stockholm 33
    4.1 Best Hotels in Stockholm 34
5. Dining and Cuisine 53
    5.1. Traditional Swedish Foods...53
    5.2. Recommended Restaurants...56
    5.3. Vegetarian and Vegan Options 56
    5.4. Cafes and Coffee Shops 57
    5.5. Swedish Fika Culture 57
6. Culture and Entertainment in Stockholm 59

- 6.1 Art Galleries..59
- 6.2 Theaters and Performing Arts 61
- 6.3 Nightlife in Stockholm..63
- 6.4 Shopping in Stockholm...65
- 7. Seasonal activities in Stockholm..............................68
  - 7.1 Summer 68
  - 7.2 Winter 70
- 8. Day Trips and Excursions 73
  - 8.1. Archipelago Cruises...73
  - 8.2. Sigtuna - Sweden's Oldest Town 73
  - 8.3. Uppsala - A Historic University City 74
  - 8.4. Drottningholm Palace and Gardens 75
  - 8.5. Viking History and Cultural Experiences........75
- 9. Stockholm 3-Day Itinerary for First Timers 77
  - Day 1 Itinerary:...77
  - Day 1 Map...79
  - Day 2 Itinerary...80
  - Day 2 Map..84
  - Day 3 Itinerary:...85
  - Day 3 Map..88
- 10. Stockolm 3-Day Travel Itinerary for Couples.......89
  - Day 1: 89
  - Day 2: 90
  - Day 3: 91
- 11. Stockholm 3-Day Itinerary For Families................94
  - Day 1:..94
  - Day 2: 95
  - Day 3: 96
- 12. Practical Information and Tips 98
  - 12.1. Currency and Money 98
  - 12.2. Tipping and Gratuity..98
  - 12.3. Electricity and Adapters 98
  - 12.4. Internet and Wi-Fi Access 98

12.5. Emergency Services and Medical Assistance 98
12.6. Local Customs and Etiquette..98
12.7. Safety and Security..99
Thank you!...100

1. Introduction

Stockholm is Sweden's capital city. Located on the south-central east coast, it is the largest city in Scandinavia, with a population of over two million people. Despite its northerly location, Stockholm has a relatively warm climate, with an average annual temperature of 10°C. In winter, the average temperature is just below 0°C, although there are times when it can drop to -15°C. In the summer, the temperature averages 18°C, with a few hotter days around 25-27°C. Daylight hours in Stockholm also vary wildly depending on what time of year you visit. In June, Stockholm sees 18 hours of daylight, while in December there are only around six hours, with both extremes having their own charm.

Stockholm itself is made up of 14 islands, connected by over 50 bridges. These islands lie next to the 30,000 islands that make up the Stockholm archipelago, spreading out into the Baltic Sea. The oldest part of the city (Gamla Stan) dates back to the 13th century, while the rest is a real mixture of designs and influences. These range from the Baroque-style royal palace, built in the 1700s, to modern architecture such as the Ericsson Globe, the largest hemispherical building in the world.

Stockholm's main feature, however, is the water and it's not hard to see why the city is sometimes referred to as "the Venice of the north".

Riddarholmen and Gamla Stan (the old town) from across the lake

Södermalm (the southern island) in winter

1.1 The History of Stockholm

Stockholm has a rich and fascinating history that spans over 700 years. The city was founded in 1252 by Birger Jarl, a Swedish statesman and military leader, and has since grown into a thriving metropolis that is home to over 1 million people.

During the Middle Ages, Stockholm grew rapidly as a center of trade and commerce. The city's location on the east coast of Sweden, on the edge of the Baltic Sea, made it a prime location for trade with other countries in the region, including Germany, Russia, and the Baltic States.

In the 14th and 15th centuries, Stockholm became the capital of Sweden and the seat of the Swedish monarchy. The city grew in size and importance, with the construction of impressive buildings and landmarks such as the Royal Palace and the Storkyrkan, the city's oldest church.

In the 16th and 17th centuries, Stockholm continued to grow and flourish, becoming a major player in European politics and culture. The city's architecture and art reflected the influences of the Renaissance and the Baroque periods, with grand palaces and public buildings being constructed throughout the city.

One of the most famous events in Stockholm's history occurred in 1628, when the Vasa, a grand warship built by the Swedish navy, sank on its maiden voyage in the harbor outside of Stockholm. The ship was salvaged over 300 years later and can now be seen at the Vasa Museum, one of the city's most popular attractions.

During the 18th and 19th centuries, Stockholm continued to evolve and modernize, with the city's population growing rapidly as people from all over Sweden and Europe came to live and work there. The city also became known for its innovation and creativity, with a thriving art and music scene that produced some of Sweden's most famous artists, writers, and musicians.

In the early 20th century, Stockholm was at the forefront of social and political change, with the city's workers and labor unions playing a key role in the struggle for workers' rights and social justice. The city was also home to important cultural movements, such as the Swedish modernist movement and the emergence of Swedish cinema as a major force in international film.

During World War II, Stockholm played a crucial role in providing aid and support to neighboring countries that had been occupied by Nazi forces. The city was also home to a large number of refugees and exiles from other parts of Europe, who found safety and shelter in Stockholm's tolerant and welcoming environment.

In the post-war period, Stockholm continued to grow and prosper, becoming a modern and cosmopolitan city with a thriving economy and a diverse population. Today, Stockholm is known for its world-class museums, stunning architecture, and innovative culture, as well as its commitment to sustainability and environmentalism.

One of the key events in Stockholm's recent history was the abolition of Sweden's monarchy in 1975, which marked a significant shift in the country's political and social landscape. Today, Stockholm is governed by a democratically elected city council and has a vibrant and active civil society that is engaged in shaping the city's future.

Despite the many changes and challenges that Stockholm has faced over the centuries, the city has remained a resilient and vibrant center of culture and creativity. From its medieval roots to its modern-day innovations, Stockholm is a city that continues to captivate and inspire visitors from around the world.

One of the ways in which Stockholm has managed to preserve its history and cultural heritage is through its numerous museums and cultural institutions. The city is home to some of the world's most impressive museums, including the Nationalmuseum, which houses an extensive collection of Swedish art and design, and the Museum of Medieval Stockholm, which offers visitors a glimpse into the city's medieval past.

Stockholm is also known for its world-class performing arts scene, with numerous theaters and concert halls hosting a wide range of performances throughout the year. The Royal Swedish Opera and the Stockholm Concert Hall are two of the city's most iconic cultural landmarks, known for their stunning architecture and world-renowned performances.

In recent years, Stockholm has also become a hub for innovation and creativity, with a thriving startup scene and a growing number of co-working spaces and incubators. The city's focus on sustainability and environmentalism has also made it a leader in sustainable urban development, with numerous green spaces and eco-friendly initiatives aimed at reducing the city's carbon footprint.

Despite its many achievements, Stockholm is not without its challenges. Like many cities around the world, Stockholm is grappling with issues such as affordable housing, social inequality, and the impact of climate change. However, the city's leaders and residents are committed to addressing these issues and creating a more sustainable and equitable future for all.

Overall, the history of Stockholm is a testament to the resilience and creativity of its people, who have managed to build and maintain a vibrant and thriving city over the course of centuries. From its medieval roots to its modern-day innovations, Stockholm continues to be a source of inspiration and wonder for visitors from around the world. Whether you're interested in history, culture, or innovation, Stockholm has something for everyone.

1.2 Stockholm's Geography and Climate

Stockholm, the capital of Sweden, is uniquely situated across 14 islands, where Lake Mälaren meets the Baltic Sea. This picturesque city is part of the Stockholm archipelago, which consists of around 30,000 islands, islets, and rocks. Due to its distinct location, Stockholm is sometimes referred to as the "Venice of the North," as its many waterways, bridges, and waterfront promenades define the city's landscape.

Geographically, Stockholm lies at 59°19′46″N latitude and 18°4′7″E longitude, occupying a total area of 188 square kilometers (73 square miles). The city's topography is relatively flat, with the highest natural point being 47 meters (154 feet) above sea level. Stockholm's terrain is characterized by a mix of rocky outcrops, green parks, and both urban and natural waterfronts.

The climate in Stockholm is classified as humid continental, with significant temperature variations between seasons. Summers are generally warm and pleasant, with average high temperatures ranging from 20°C to 25°C (68°F to 77°F) in June, July, and August. This is the best time to visit Stockholm, as the days are long, with up to 18 hours of daylight, and the city comes alive with outdoor activities, events, and al fresco dining.

Winters in Stockholm are cold and dark, with temperatures ranging from -6°C to 1°C (21°F to 34°F) between December and February. Snow is common during these months, creating a picturesque winter wonderland in the city. However, daylight hours can be as short as 6 hours during this time, making outdoor sightseeing more limited.

The shoulder seasons of spring (April and May) and autumn (September and October) offer milder temperatures, fewer crowds, and more affordable accommodation options. While the weather can be unpredictable during these months, with rain or even snow, it's a great time to experience Stockholm's changing seasons and natural beauty.

When planning a trip to Stockholm, it's essential to pack appropriate clothing for the climate, including layers for fluctuating temperatures, waterproof shoes, and a rain jacket or umbrella to handle the city's frequent rain showers.

1.3. Swedish Language and Culture

Swedish Language:
Swedish is the official language of Sweden and is spoken by the majority of the population. It belongs to the North Germanic language family, which also includes Norwegian, Danish, Icelandic, and Faroese. Swedish is closely

related to Norwegian and Danish, and speakers of these languages can generally understand one another.

While Swedish is the primary language in Stockholm, the city is quite cosmopolitan and most people, especially those working in the tourism and service industries, can speak English fluently. However, learning a few basic Swedish phrases can go a long way in making your stay more enjoyable and showing respect for the local culture. Some helpful phrases include:

Hej (Hey): Hello
Tack (Tack): Thank you
Snälla (Snella): Please
Förlåt (Fur-lawt): Excuse me / Sorry
Ja (Ya): Yes
Nej (Nay): No
God morgon (Good mor-gon): Good morning
God kväll (Good kvell): Good evening
Hej då (Hey doe): Goodbye

Swedish Culture:
Swedish culture is characterized by a strong sense of community, equality, and environmental consciousness. The concept of "lagom," which translates to "just the right amount," is deeply ingrained in Swedish society and emphasizes moderation, balance, and a focus on what truly matters.

Sweden has a rich history of design, art, and architecture, which is evident in Stockholm's well-preserved buildings, sleek interiors, and world-class museums. Swedish design is known for its minimalism, functionality, and attention to detail, which can be seen in everything from furniture to fashion.

The Swedes also take great pride in their culinary heritage, with traditional dishes like meatballs, herring, and gravlax playing an essential role in their cuisine. The custom of "fika" (a coffee break with pastries and socializing) is an important daily ritual, reflecting the Swedish appreciation for taking time to relax and enjoy life's simple pleasures.

Outdoor activities are popular in Stockholm, as Swedes have a deep connection with nature and embrace the concept of "friluftsliv" (open-air living). Whether it's strolling through the city's many parks, ice-skating on frozen lakes, or exploring the nearby archipelago, experiencing Stockholm's natural beauty is an integral part of the local culture.

When visiting Stockholm, it's essential to be respectful of local customs and values. This includes being punctual, as the Swedes place a high importance on time management, and being mindful of personal space and privacy.

1.4 10 Must-Know Swedish Personalities from History

III. 10 Must-Know Swedish Personalities from History

Sweden has a rich history and has produced a number of influential and noteworthy individuals over the years. Here are ten must-know Swedish personalities from various fields, including arts, culture, government, music, science, and more.

1. **Carl Linnaeus** (1707-1778) Carl Linnaeus was a Swedish botanist and zoologist who is known as the father of modern taxonomy. His groundbreaking work in classifying and naming plants and animals laid the foundation for modern biology and helped to establish Sweden as a center of scientific excellence.

2. **August Strindberg** (1849-1912) August Strindberg was a Swedish playwright, novelist, and essayist who is considered one of the most important figures in modern Swedish literature. His works, which include plays such as "Miss Julie" and "The Dance of Death," are known for their psychological depth and exploration of complex human emotions.

3. **Ingmar Bergman** (1918-2007) Ingmar Bergman was a Swedish film director and screenwriter who is regarded as one of the greatest filmmakers of all time. His films, which include "The Seventh Seal" and "Wild Strawberries," are known for their philosophical themes, stunning visuals, and innovative storytelling techniques.

4. **Raoul Wallenberg** (1912-unknown) Raoul Wallenberg was a Swedish diplomat who is credited with saving the lives of thousands of Jews during the Holocaust. He used his diplomatic status to issue protective passports and shelter Jews in safe houses, risking his own life in the process. Wallenberg's fate remains unknown, as he disappeared after being arrested by Soviet forces in 1945.

5. **Alfred Nobel** (1833-1896) Alfred Nobel was a Swedish chemist, engineer, and inventor who is best known for his invention of dynamite. He also established the Nobel Prizes, which are awarded annually for achievements in physics, chemistry, medicine, literature, and peace.

6. **Greta Garbo** (1905-1990) Greta Garbo was a Swedish-American actress who is considered one of the greatest screen actresses of all time. She appeared in numerous Hollywood films during the 1920s and 1930s, including "Grand Hotel" and "Ninotchka," and was known for her iconic beauty and enigmatic personality.

7. **Olof Palme** (1927-1986) Olof Palme was a Swedish politician who served as the country's prime minister for two non-consecutive terms. He was known for his progressive policies, including his strong support for disarmament and his opposition to apartheid in South Africa. Palme was assassinated in 1986, and his killer remains unknown.

8. **ABBA** (active 1972-1983) ABBA was a Swedish pop group that achieved worldwide success during the 1970s and 1980s. The group, which consisted of Agnetha Fältskog, Björn Ulvaeus, Benny Andersson, and Anni-Frid Lyngstad, is known for hits such as "Dancing Queen" and "Mamma Mia!" and is considered one of the most successful musical acts of all time.

9. **Astrid Lindgren** (1907-2002) Astrid Lindgren was a Swedish author and screenwriter who is best known for her children's books, including the popular Pippi Longstocking series. Her books have been translated into over 100 languages and have sold over 165 million copies worldwide.

10. **Anders Celsius** (1701-1744) Anders Celsius was a Swedish astronomer and mathematician who is credited with developing the Celsius temperature scale, which is used in most of the world today. Celsius also made significant contributions to the field of astronomy, including the discovery of the aurora borealis.

These ten Swedish personalities represent just a small sample of the many influential and noteworthy individuals who have come from this country. From science to the arts, government to music, Sweden has produced a wide range of talented and visionary individuals who have left their mark on the world. By learning about these individuals and their contributions, we can gain a deeper understanding of Swedish history and culture and appreciate the many ways in which Sweden has helped to shape the world we live in today.

1.5 Top Attractions in Stockholm

Stockholm is home to a wealth of top attractions, ranging from historic landmarks to world-renowned museums. Here's a list of the must-see sights in Stockholm:

1. Gamla Stan (Old Town)

Gamla Stan is the historic heart of Stockholm, featuring cobblestone streets, medieval architecture, and numerous shops, restaurants, and cafes. This charming district is home to several key attractions, including the Royal Palace and the Nobel Museum.

Visitor Information:
- Opening Hours: Open daily, but hours vary depending on individual shops and restaurants.
- Ticket Price: Free to explore, but some attractions may charge an admission fee.
- Website: https://www.visitstockholm.com/see--do/attractions/gamla-stan-old-town/

2. Vasa Museum

The Vasa Museum is home to the world's only preserved 17th-century ship, the Vasa. This impressive vessel sank on its maiden voyage in 1628 and was salvaged in the 1960s. The museum features exhibits on the ship's history and restoration, as well as interactive displays and workshops.

Visitor Information:
- Opening Hours: Open daily from 10 am to 5 pm, with extended hours on Wednesdays until 8 pm.
- Ticket Price: 170 SEK (approximately $20 USD) for adults, free for children under 18.
- Website: https://www.vasamuseet.se/en

3. Skansen Open-Air Museum

Skansen is an open-air museum and zoo that showcases Swedish culture and history. The museum features more than 150 historic buildings, including farmhouses, workshops, and windmills. Visitors can also explore the zoo, which is home to a variety of Nordic animals such as bears, moose, and wolves.

Visitor Information:
- Opening Hours: Open daily, but hours vary depending on the season.
- Ticket Price: 230 SEK (approximately $27 USD) for adults, 130 SEK (approximately $15 USD) for children ages 4-15.
- Website: https://www.skansen.se/en/

4. ABBA The Museum

ABBA The Museum is dedicated to the iconic Swedish pop group, ABBA. The museum features exhibits on the group's history, costumes, and music, as well as interactive displays where visitors can sing and dance along to their favorite ABBA songs.

Visitor Information:
- Opening Hours: Open daily from 10 am to 6 pm.
- Ticket Price: 250 SEK (approximately $29 USD) for adults, 95 SEK (approximately $11 USD) for children ages 7-15.
- Website: https://www.abbathemuseum.com/en/

5. Djurgården Island

Djurgården Island is a popular destination for locals and visitors alike, featuring beautiful parks, museums, and attractions. The island is home to several key sights, including the Skansen Open-Air Museum, ABBA The Museum, and the Vasa Museum.

Visitor Information:
- Opening Hours: Open daily, but hours vary depending on individual attractions.
- Ticket Price: Prices vary depending on individual attractions.
- Website: https://www.visitstockholm.com/see--do/attractions/djurgarden/

6. Royal Palace of Stockholm

The Royal Palace of Stockholm is the official residence of the Swedish royal family. Visitors can explore the palace's impressive rooms and halls, including the Royal Apartments and the Treasury, which houses the royal family's crown jewels.

Visitor Information:
- Opening Hours: Open daily from 10 am to 5 pm, with extended hours in the summer.
- Ticket Price: 160 SEK (approximately $19 USD) for adults, free for children under 18.
- Website: https://www.kungligaslotten.se/english.html

7. Stockholm City Hall

Stockholm City Hall is a magnificent building located on the waterfront, known for its grand architecture and ornate interior. Visitors can take guided tours of the building and visit the famous Golden Hall, which features a stunning mosaic made of over 18 million pieces of gold leaf.

Visitor Information:
- Opening Hours: Open daily for guided tours, with varying hours depending on the season.

- Ticket Price: 120 SEK (approximately $14 USD) for adults, 60 SEK (approximately $7 USD) for children ages 7-19.
- Website: https://www.stockholm.se/en/organisation/stockholm-city-hall/

8. Fotografiska Stockholm

Fotografiska Stockholm is a contemporary photography museum that showcases both Swedish and international photographers. The museum features rotating exhibits, workshops, and events, as well as a café and restaurant with stunning waterfront views.

Visitor Information:
- Opening Hours: Open daily, with varying hours depending on the season.
- Ticket Price: 170 SEK (approximately $20 USD) for adults, free for children under 12.
- Website: https://www.fotografiska.com/sto/en/

9. Moderna Museet

Moderna Museet is one of Scandinavia's leading museums of modern and contemporary art. The museum features a diverse collection of works from the 20th century to the present day, including pieces by famous artists such as Pablo Picasso, Salvador Dali, and Andy Warhol.

Visitor Information:
- Opening Hours: Open daily, with varying hours depending on the season.
- Ticket Price: Free admission, but some special exhibits may charge an admission fee.
- Website: https://www.modernamuseet.se/stockholm/en/

10. Nationalmuseum

Nationalmuseum is Sweden's largest art museum, featuring a collection of over 700,000 works of art from the Middle Ages to the 20th century. The museum's impressive collection includes paintings, sculptures, and decorative arts from around the world.

Visitor Information:
- Opening Hours: Open daily, with varying hours depending on the season.
- Ticket Price: Free admission to the permanent collection, but some special exhibits may charge an admission fee.
- Website: https://www.nationalmuseum.se/en/visit

These top attractions in Stockholm are just a small sample of what the city has to offer. No matter what your interests are, there is something for everyone in Stockholm.

1.6 When to Visit Stockholm

Stockholm is a city that can be enjoyed year-round, with each season offering its own unique experiences. However, the best time to visit depends on your interests, budget, and preferred weather conditions.

Shoulder Season:
The shoulder season in Stockholm runs from April to May and from September to October. During this time, the crowds are smaller, the weather is milder, and the prices for accommodations and activities are lower. The average temperature during these months ranges from 6°C to 15°C (43°F to 59°F), and there are typically fewer rainy days than in the summer months.

Low Season:
The low season in Stockholm runs from November to March. During this time, the weather is colder, and the days are shorter. However, this is also a great time to visit if you're interested in winter sports, Christmas markets, or the Northern Lights. The average temperature during these months ranges from -3°C to 3°C (27°F to 37°F), and there are typically more rainy and snowy days.

High Season:
The high season in Stockholm runs from June to August. During this time, the weather is warm, and the days are long. However, this is also the most crowded and expensive time to visit, with many tourists flocking to the city to enjoy the summer festivals, outdoor activities, and long hours of sunlight. The average temperature during these months ranges from 16°C to 22°C (61°F to 72°F), and there are typically more sunny days with occasional rain.

Here's a more detailed monthly breakdown of the weather in Stockholm:
- January: Average temperature ranges from -4°C to 0°C (25°F to 32°F). Snowfall is common, and there are around 15 rainy/snowy days.
- February: Average temperature ranges from -4°C to 1°C (25°F to 34°F). Snowfall is common, and there are around 11 rainy/snowy days.
- March: Average temperature ranges from 0°C to 5°C (32°F to 41°F). There may be some snow, but the weather starts to get milder, and there are around 10 rainy days.
- April: Average temperature ranges from 3°C to 10°C (37°F to 50°F). The weather is mild, but there are still some rainy days.
- May: Average temperature ranges from 8°C to 15°C (46°F to 59°F). The weather is mild and sunny, with occasional rain showers.
- June: Average temperature ranges from 13°C to 20°C (55°F to 68°F). The weather is warm and sunny, with occasional rain showers.
- July: Average temperature ranges from 16°C to 23°C (61°F to 73°F). The weather is warm and sunny, with occasional rain showers.
- August: Average temperature ranges from 15°C to 22°C (59°F to 72°F). The weather is warm and sunny, with occasional rain showers.

- September: Average temperature ranges from 10°C to 16°C (50°F to 61°F). The weather is mild and sunny, with occasional rain showers.
- October: Average temperature ranges from 5°C to 10°C (41°F to 50°F). The weather is mild, but there are more rainy days.
- November: Average temperature ranges from 1°C to 5°C (34°F to 41°F). There may be some snow and rain, and the days are getting shorter.
- December: Average temperature ranges from -2°C to 1°C (28°F to 34°F). There may be some snow and rain, and the days are short.

No matter what time of year you visit Stockholm, there are plenty of things to see and do. During the summer months, the city comes alive with festivals, outdoor concerts, and events such as Midsummer celebrations and the Stockholm Pride Parade. The beaches and parks around the city are also popular with locals and visitors alike.

In the winter months, you can experience the magic of the holiday season with Christmas markets, ice-skating rinks, and cozy cafes and restaurants. Stockholm is also a great destination for winter sports, such as skiing, snowboarding, and ice-skating.

If you're looking to avoid the crowds and save some money, the shoulder season or low season can be a great time to visit. You'll still be able to experience the city's attractions and activities, but with fewer people and lower prices.

No matter when you visit, it's important to pack accordingly for the weather. During the summer months, light clothing and comfortable walking shoes are recommended, while in the winter months, warm clothing, boots, and a waterproof jacket are essential.

Overall, Stockholm is a city that can be enjoyed year-round, with something to offer every type of traveler. Whether you're interested in history, culture, outdoor activities, or just soaking up the local atmosphere, Stockholm is sure to delight and inspire you.

1.7 FAQs: travelling to Stockholm

What is the time zone in Stockholm?
Sweden uses Central European Time (CET), which is GMT+1. During daylight savings time, Central European Summer Time (CEST) is used, GMT+2.

What is the currency in Sweden?
The currency in Sweden is the Swedish krona.

Should I use cash or credit card?
Stockholm is an almost completely cashless society. Be aware that there are some places that will not accept cash; it is unlikely that you will need cash when travelling in Stockholm, even taxis and vending machines accept credit cards. Tips can also be given using credit card, although there is not a big tipping culture. It is typical to just round up the bill if you feel the service has been good. If you do wish to use cash, there are ATMs and foreign exchanges available throughout the city.

Is Stockholm a safe city?
Like many Nordic cities, Stockholm is generally very safe. Just use usual common sense, looking out for your personal belongings when in crowded places and stay aware of your surroundings.

Will I need an adapter plug for my electrical appliances?
As with most of Europe, Sweden uses the Type C electrical plug (Europlug).

What is the best time of year to visit Stockholm?
Stockholm is very different depending on what time of year it is. Most people will say the best time of year to visit Stockholm is June to August, when it is warm and sunny, however, it is also very beautiful in winter. It is really dependent on what type of holiday you want and what in Stockholm you want to see and do. There is a seasonal guide to activities in Stockholm further on in this book.

What clothes should I bring with me?
People in Stockholm are typically quite stylish but favour muted colours. If you want to fit in with the crowd, keep it simple with black, white and grey. Due to its proximity to the water, Stockholm can be quite breezy, so even in summer it's best to have layers to keep warm. In winter it's important to wrap up with a good winter jacket, hat and gloves. The pavements can be quite slushy and icy so make sure you bring a pair of sturdy winter boots.

Can I use my SL travel card to travel to the airport?
If you are traveling to Bromma airport it is possible to use SL public transport and therefore your SL travel card. However, SL travel cards are not valid on airport coaches or the Arlanda Express. You can use the regular

commuter rail service to reach Arlanda airport using your SL travel card, however you must pay a supplement of SEK 120. The journey takes approximately 40 minutes.

2. Getting To Stockholm

There are three airports in the vicinity of Stockholm: Arlanda, Bromma and Skavsta. Which one you fly to will most likely depend on the airline you choose to fly with and from where you start your journey.

1. Arlanda airport

Arlanda airport (ARN) is Stockholm's main airport and the largest of the three; be aware that there are four terminals at Arlanda airport.
Arlanda is roughly 40km (25 miles) away from Stockholm city centre, but the transport links into town are excellent and there are screens up in the arrivals areas showing departure times for busses and trains.

If you are less than five people, the cheapest way to get into the city centre is by airport coach (Flygbussarna). There are several routes available depending on where you are staying, but it takes around 45 minutes to reach the city centre. If you buy online or via the app, an adult, single ticket costs SEK 99 (usually SEK 119). The ticket is valid for three months from the time of purchase. Tickets can also be bought from ticket machines at the airport, at the shops 7-Eleven and Pressbyrån or on-board the bus itself, although be aware that bus drivers will not accept cash. Timetables and bus routes can be found on the airport coaches website in several languages. Flygbussarna also operate a door-to-gate service, which is essentially a shared taxi with room for up to 9 people in each minibus. This can be a more convenient way to travel than getting the bus, while being cheaper than a private taxi. Pricing examples can be found on the website, however, for trips to the city centre it costs SEK 289 for the first person and then SEK 65 for every additional person in your booking, meaning for a couple it would cost SEK 354.

The fastest way into central Stockholm is the Arlanda Express train, which takes around 20 minutes. An adult, single ticket costs SEK 280, although there are often discounts online for groups or those booking far in advance, so it is worth checking the website to see if you can get a better price. Children under 18 can travel for free when accompanied by an adult over 25.

A taxi from Arlanda into the city centre can take around 40 minutes. Taxi prices in Sweden are not regulated, so always confirm the price with the driver before you set off. You do not need to take the first taxi in the queue at the taxi rank if the price doesn't suit you. The major taxi companies such as Taxi Stockholm, Sverige Taxi and Taxi Kurir have fixed prices between Arlanda and the city centre of around SEK 450-500. Remember to always ask the driver about the cost and to check the taxi pricing, which can be found on a yellow label in the taxi window. Taxis will also accept credit cards although you can pay with cash if preferred.

2. Skavsta airport

Skavsta airport (NYO) is the furthest airport of the three, however it is the airport most often flown to by budget airlines. It is roughly 100km (62 miles) southwest of Stockholm.

The easiest way to get to Stockholm from Skavsta airport is by airport coach. An adult, single ticket costs SEK 139 and takes around 80 minutes. If you can't face that long on a coach, then taxi takes around 70 minutes and should cost between SEK 1,500 and SEK 2,000.

3. Bromma airport
Bromma airport (BMA) is the closest airport to Stockholm city. It mostly has domestic flights, but a small number of international flights also fly from here. It is around 7km (just over 4 miles) away from the city centre. As ever, the airport coach is the easiest way to get into the city, with an adult, single ticket costing SEK 75. The journey itself takes only 20 minutes. If you want to save some money, it is possible to travel to and from the airport using the regular public transport. This is more or less convenient depending on where in the city you are staying. The best way to find a route is using the SL journey planner.

2.1. Flights and Airports

Stockholm is well-connected to various international destinations via its primary airport, Stockholm Arlanda Airport (ARN). Located about 40 kilometers (25 miles) north of the city center, Arlanda Airport is the largest and busiest airport in Sweden, serving more than 25 million passengers annually.

Major airlines operating at Arlanda Airport include SAS (Scandinavian Airlines), Norwegian Air Shuttle, Lufthansa, British Airways, Air France, KLM, and Emirates, among others. They offer direct flights from numerous cities across Europe, Asia, North America, and the Middle East. For specific flight schedules and prices, it is recommended to visit the respective airline websites or use popular flight search engines like Skyscanner (https://www.skyscanner.net/) or Google Flights (https://www.google.com/flights/).

Stockholm also has a few smaller airports, including Stockholm Bromma Airport (BMA), Stockholm Skavsta Airport (NYO), and Stockholm Västerås Airport (VST). These airports mostly serve domestic and low-cost European flights operated by airlines such as Ryanair, Wizz Air, and BRA (Braathens Regional Airlines). Prices and schedules for these airlines can be found on their official websites or the aforementioned flight search engines.

Upon arrival at Arlanda Airport, there are several transportation options to reach Stockholm's city center:

1. **Arlanda Express:** The fastest way to reach the city center is by taking the Arlanda Express train, which takes approximately 20 minutes. Tickets can be purchased online (https://www.arlandaexpress.com/), at the airport's ticket machines, or onboard the train. Prices for a one-way adult ticket range from 299 SEK (approximately $32) when booked in advance, up to 350 SEK (approximately $37) when purchased at the airport or onboard. Discounts are available for students, seniors, and groups.
2. **Commuter Trains (Pendeltåg):** A more affordable alternative is the commuter train, which takes around 40 minutes to reach the city center. Tickets can be purchased at the airport's SL Center or via the SL app (https://www.sl.se/en/). The price for a one-way ticket, including the airport access fee, is approximately 152 SEK (around $16) for adults and 104 SEK (around $11) for children and youth.
3. **Flygbussarna Airport Coaches:** The Flygbussarna buses offer a comfortable and budget-friendly option, taking about 45 minutes to reach the city center. Tickets can be purchased online (https://www.flygbussarna.se/en), at the airport's ticket machines, or onboard the bus with a credit card. Prices for a one-way adult ticket are 119 SEK (approximately $13) when booked online, and 139 SEK (approximately $15) when purchased at the airport or onboard. Discounts are available for students, seniors, and children.

4. **Taxis and Ridesharing:** Taxis and ridesharing services like Uber and Bolt are available at the airport, with a typical fare to the city center costing around 450-600 SEK (approximately $48-$64) depending on the time of day and traffic. Always confirm the price with the driver before starting the trip, as taxi fares can vary.

For detailed information on transportation options, visit the Stockholm Arlanda Airport website (https://www.swedavia.com/arlanda/).

2.2. Train and Bus Connections

Stockholm is well-connected to other Swedish cities and neighboring countries via an extensive network of trains and buses. The primary train and bus station in the city is Stockholm Central Station (Stockholms Centralstation), which serves as a hub for regional and international connections.

Trains:
1. SJ (Statens Järnvägar) is Sweden's largest train operator, offering high-speed and regional train services within Sweden and to neighboring countries such as Norway and Denmark. Popular domestic routes include Gothenburg, Malmö, and Uppsala. International routes include Oslo (Norway) and Copenhagen (Denmark). For schedules, ticket prices, and bookings, visit the SJ website (https://www.sj.se/en/).
2. Snälltåget provides seasonal direct train services from Stockholm to Malmö, Copenhagen, and Berlin (Germany), as well as popular ski destinations in Sweden during the winter months. For more information, visit the Snälltåget website (https://www.snalltaget.se/en).
3. MTRX is another train operator offering high-speed services between Stockholm and Gothenburg. Visit the MTRX website for schedules and ticket prices (https://www.mtr.se/en).

Buses:
1. FlixBus is a popular low-cost bus operator with extensive routes across Sweden and Europe. They offer frequent and affordable connections between Stockholm and other Swedish cities, as well as international destinations such as Oslo, Copenhagen, Berlin, and Prague. For more information, visit the FlixBus website (https://www.flixbus.com/).
2. Nettbuss Bus4You provides comfortable bus services within Sweden, including popular routes such as Stockholm to Gothenburg, Malmö, and Karlstad. For schedules and prices, visit the Nettbuss website (https://www.nettbuss.se/en).

2.3. Cruise and Ferry Services

Stockholm's strategic location on the Baltic Sea makes it a popular port of call for cruise ships and ferries. The city's main cruise terminals are

Frihamnen, Värtahamnen, and Stadsgården, which welcome numerous international cruise lines such as Royal Caribbean, Norwegian Cruise Line, and Viking Cruises.

Ferries:
1. Viking Line operates daily ferry services between Stockholm and Helsinki (Finland), Turku (Finland), and Tallinn (Estonia). These overnight ferries provide a comfortable and scenic way to explore the Baltic Sea and visit neighboring countries. Prices and schedules can be found on the Viking Line website (https://www.sales.vikingline.com/).
2. Tallink Silja Line offers daily ferry services from Stockholm to Helsinki, Turku, Tallinn, and Riga (Latvia). The ferries feature various onboard amenities, including restaurants, bars, entertainment, and shopping. For more information on routes, schedules, and prices, visit the Tallink Silja Line website (https://www.tallinksilja.com/en).
3. St. Peter Line operates a ferry service between Stockholm and St. Petersburg (Russia) with a stop in Helsinki. This route offers a convenient way to visit Russia without a visa for up to 72 hours. Visit the St. Peter Line website for schedules and prices (https://stpeterline.com/en/).

It is important to note that schedules and prices for trains, buses, and ferries may vary depending on the season and availability. Always book your tickets in advance to ensure the best prices and confirm travel details.

2.4. Visa Requirements and Entry Regulations

Sweden is a member of the European Union (EU) and the Schengen Area, which allows for the free movement of people between its 26 member countries. Visa requirements and entry regulations for visiting Stockholm depend on your nationality and the duration of your stay.

1. EU/EEA and Swiss Citizens: If you are a citizen of an EU/EEA country or Switzerland, you do not need a visa to enter Sweden for short stays (up to 90 days in any 180-day period). You only need a valid passport or national ID card to travel. For longer stays, EU/EEA and Swiss citizens have the right to live and work in Sweden without a visa but may need to register with the Swedish Migration Agency (Migrationsverket) if staying for more than three months.

2. Non-EU/EEA and Non-Swiss Citizens: For citizens of non-EU/EEA countries and those not eligible for visa-free travel, visa requirements vary depending on your nationality:

- Visa-exempt countries: Citizens of several countries, including the United States, Canada, Australia, and Japan, do not need a visa for short stays in the Schengen Area (up to 90 days in any 180-day period) for tourism, family visits, or business purposes. You must have a valid passport with at least three months' validity beyond your planned departure date from the Schengen Area.

- Visa-required countries: Citizens of countries that do not have a visa waiver agreement with the Schengen Area must apply for a Schengen visa before traveling to Sweden. This includes countries such as India, China, and South Africa. To apply for a Schengen visa, you need to submit your application at the Swedish embassy or consulate in your country of residence. The process usually involves providing documentation related to your trip, such as travel itinerary, accommodation bookings, and proof of financial means, as well as paying a visa fee.

Please note that entry regulations and visa requirements may change, so it is always important to consult the official website of the Swedish Migration Agency (https://www.migrationsverket.se/English/Private-individuals/Visiting-Sweden.html) or the nearest Swedish embassy or consulate for the most up-to-date information before planning your trip.

In addition to visa requirements, all travelers to Stockholm should be aware of current health and safety regulations, such as COVID-19 testing and quarantine requirements, which may vary depending on your country of origin and the current situation. For the latest information on entry requirements and health regulations, visit the Swedish Public Health Agency website (https://www.folkhalsomyndigheten.se/the-public-health-agency-of-sweden/) and the Swedish Police Authority website (https://polisen.se/en/the-swedish-police/the-coronavirus-and-the-swedish-police/).

3. Getting Around Stockholm

The best way to get around Stockholm is by using the extensive public transport system, including busses, trains, metro, trams and ferries. While this may sound complicated it is actually relatively easy to navigate your way around as most of the public transport is run by one company, SL. This makes it incredibly simple when buying tickets or using the journey planner (which is also available in English).

Unless you're sure you really want to walk around the city for your entire trip you are best to buy an SL travel card. Tickets for individual journeys can be purchased, but they are relatively expensive (SEK 44, valid for 70 minutes) and it soon adds up to be cheaper with a travel card. A 72-hour travel card costs SEK 250 for an adult. Travel cards can be bought at metro stations or in shops that display the SL logo such as 7-eleven and Pressbyrån (these shops can also be found at Arlanda airport). The SL travel card is valid on most transport in Stockholm with the exception of some boats operated by Waxholmsbolaget. You must pay for your ticket before attempting to use public transport.

Artwork in the metro station (photo by Johannes Hurtig on Unsplash)

It is also possible to buy a Stockholm Pass, which includes the cost of the SL travel card as well as free entry to many of the city's largest tourist attractions and a guide book. A three-day Stockholm Pass plus SL travel card costs SEK 1295 for one adult, although there are often discounts available on their website. The pass can be bought online and delivered to you (at a cost of up to SEK 80) before you leave for Stockholm, or alternatively you can pick it up when you arrive, but this involves heading to one of the redemption desks situated in town. It is also possible to download the pass to your mobile phone, which is probably the most convenient method to use. If you want to wait until you're in Stockholm, there are also several places where you can buy the Stockholm Pass directly. If you intend to do all the activities in this guide, and only these activities, and to travel via public transport throughout the three days, then it is around SEK 10 more expensive to use the Stockholm Pass than to buy each ticket separately. The best way to decide whether or not to buy a Stockholm Pass is to plan what you want to see and work out the individual costs. If you plan on doing a lot of sightseeing then it can offer really great value, however if you are more interested in relaxing and enjoying the restaurants then it might not be worth it.

Useful contact and travel information
Stockholm's airports: +46 10 109 10 00 Flygbussarna (airport coaches): www.flygbussarna.se/en
Arlanda Express: www.arlandaexpress.com/
Taxi Stockholm: +46 8 15 00 00, www.taxistockholm.se/en/
Taxi Kurir: +46 8 30 00 00, www.taxikurir.se/stockholm
Sverige Taxi: +46 8 85 04 00, www.sverigetaxi.se/
Stockholm visitors centre: +46 8 508 285 08, www.visitstockholm.com/
SL journey planner: https://sl.se/en/

3.1. Public Transportation
Stockholm has an efficient and comprehensive public transportation system operated by Storstockholms Lokaltrafik (SL). The system includes the subway (Tunnelbana), buses, trams, and commuter trains (Pendeltåg), making it easy and convenient to explore the city and its surrounding areas.

3.1.1. Subway (Tunnelbana)
The Tunnelbana is Stockholm's subway system, with seven lines (T10, T11, T13, T14, T17, T18, and T19) connecting 100 stations across the city. The subway is color-coded, with blue, red, and green lines, and is known for its uniquely designed stations, often featuring impressive artwork and sculptures. Operating hours vary depending on the line, with trains running from around 5:00 am until 1:00 am on weekdays and 24 hours on weekends (with reduced frequency during late-night hours).

3.1.2. Buses and Trams
Stockholm's extensive network of buses and trams complements the subway system and provides convenient connections to areas not served by the Tunnelbana. The buses operate on various routes throughout the city and suburbs, while trams run on the Djurgården line (7) and Lidingö line (21). The inner-city buses are blue, and the suburban buses are red. The SL website (https://www.sl.se/en/) provides route maps and timetables for both the subway and buses.

Prices and Tickets:

The same tickets and travel cards can be used on all SL-operated subway, buses, trams, and commuter trains within Stockholm County. Tickets cannot be purchased onboard the subway, trams, or commuter trains, so make sure to buy your ticket before traveling. You can purchase tickets using the SL app, at ticket machines, or at SL Centers and authorized retailers.

Some ticket options include:
1. **Single Journey Ticket:** Prices vary depending on the type of ticket (adult, youth, or senior) and the number of zones traveled. The base fare for a single journey within the city is 38 SEK (approximately $4) for adults and 26 SEK (approximately $2.80) for youth/seniors. Tickets are valid for 75-120 minutes, depending on the number of zones.
2. **Travelcard:** A Travelcard offers unlimited travel on all SL-operated public transportation for a specified period (24 hours, 72 hours, or 7 days). Prices are as follows:
   - 24-hour Travelcard: 130 SEK (approx. $14) for adults, 90 SEK (approx. $9.60) for youth/seniors
   - 72-hour Travelcard: 260 SEK (approx. $28) for adults, 180 SEK (approx. $19.20) for youth/seniors
   - 7-day Travelcard: 335 SEK (approx. $36) for adults, 225 SEK (approx. $24) for youth/seniors
3. **SL Access Card:** The SL Access Card is a reusable smart card that can be loaded with credit (pay-as-you-go) or a Travelcard. You can purchase an SL Access Card at SL Centers, ticket machines, or authorized retailers for a 20 SEK (approx. $2) fee.

Tips:
1. Children under the age of 7 travel for free when accompanied by an adult.
2. If you plan to visit multiple attractions, consider purchasing the Stockholm Pass (https://www.stockholmpass.com/), which includes free admission to over 60 attractions and museums, as well as unlimited use of public transportation (if you select the option with Travelcard). The Stockholm Pass is available for 1, 2, 3, or 5 days, with prices starting at 719 SEK (approx. $77) for adults and 359 SEK (approx. $38.50) for children.
3. Stockholm is a bike-friendly city with numerous dedicated bike lanes and paths. Consider renting a bike for a day or using the city's bike-sharing program, Stockholm City Bikes (https://www.citybikes.se/en), to explore the city at your own pace.
4. Download the SL app (https://www.sl.se/en/app/) for easy access to route maps, timetables, and real-time departure information. The app also allows you to buy tickets and plan your journey using the integrated trip planner.
5. During peak hours, public transportation can be crowded, so be prepared for limited seating and allow extra time for your journey.

6. Keep in mind that eating and drinking (except for water) are generally not allowed on the subway, buses, or trams.
7. Don't forget to validate your SL Access Card by holding it against the card reader at the start of each journey. Failure to do so may result in a fine if you are checked by a ticket inspector.

3.1.3. Commuter Trains (Pendeltåg)
Pendeltåg, or commuter trains, are an integral part of Stockholm's public transportation system. They connect the city center with suburbs and nearby towns, making it convenient for visitors to explore the wider Stockholm region.

There are four main commuter train lines: Line 40 (Märsta–Södertälje), Line 41 (Uppsala–Älvsjö), Line 42 (Bålsta–Nynäshamn), and Line 43 (Gnesta–Kungsängen). The central hub for commuter trains is Stockholm Central Station (Stockholms Centralstation), with trains running approximately every 15 minutes during peak hours and every 30 minutes during off-peak hours.

Tickets for commuter trains are the same as for other SL-operated public transportation options (subway, buses, and trams) and can be purchased via the SL app, at ticket machines, or at SL Centers and authorized retailers. The SL Access Card can also be used on commuter trains.

3.2. Biking in Stockholm
Stockholm is an ideal city for cycling, thanks to its numerous bike lanes, parks, and waterfront paths. Many of the city's attractions can be easily reached by bike, making it a fun and eco-friendly way to explore.
1. **Bike Rentals:** Several bike rental shops are available throughout the city, offering a variety of bicycles for hourly or daily rentals. Some popular bike rental companies include Stockholm City Bikes (https://www.citybikes.se/en) and Rent a Bike Stockholm (https://www.rentabikestockholm.com/). Prices vary depending on the rental duration and type of bike, but expect to pay around 250 SEK (approx. $27) for a full-day rental.
2. **Bike Sharing:** Stockholm City Bikes is the city's bike-sharing program, with over 140 stations across the city. A 3-day pass costs 165 SEK (approx. $17.70), while a season pass costs 300 SEK (approx. $32). Bikes can be used for up to 3 hours at a time and can be returned to any station.

3.3. Taxis and Ridesharing Services
Taxis are readily available in Stockholm, but they can be quite expensive compared to public transportation. It is important to note that taxi fares in Sweden are not regulated, so prices can vary significantly between

companies. Always use a reputable taxi company such as **Taxi Stockholm** (https://www.taxistockholm.se/en/), **Taxi Kurir** (https://www.taxikurir.se/en), or **SverigeTaxi** (https://sverigetaxi.se/). To avoid surprises, ask for an estimated fare before starting your journey.

Ridesharing services like **Uber** (https://www.uber.com/global/en/cities/stockholm/) and **Bolt** (https://bolt.eu/cities/stockholm/) are also available in Stockholm and can be a convenient alternative to traditional taxis. Fares are generally lower than taxis, and payments are handled through the respective apps, making it a cashless and hassle-free experience. Keep in mind that during peak hours or high-demand periods, ridesharing prices may surge, making public transportation a more cost-effective option.

3.4. Car Rentals and Driving

Renting a car in Stockholm can offer the flexibility and convenience to explore the city and its surroundings at your own pace. Major car rental companies, such as Hertz (https://www.hertz.com/rentacar/location/sweden/stockholm/), Avis (https://www.avis.com/en/locations/se/stockholm), Europcar (https://www.europcar.com/en/stations/sweden/stockholm), and Sixt (https://www.sixt.com/car-rental/sweden/stockholm/), have offices at the airports and throughout the city.

However, driving in Stockholm may not be the most practical option for everyone, as the city has an extensive and efficient public transportation system. Additionally, parking can be expensive and difficult to find, and the city center has congestion charges during peak hours. If you decide to rent a car, be sure to familiarize yourself with Swedish driving laws and regulations.

3.5. Walking and Accessibility

Stockholm is a beautiful and walkable city, with many pedestrian-friendly areas, parks, and waterfront promenades. Exploring the city on foot is not only a great way to experience its charm but also an eco-friendly and budget-friendly option. Many of the city's top attractions, such as the Old Town (Gamla Stan), Royal Palace, and Djurgården Island, can be easily reached on foot.

The city is generally accessible for people with disabilities, with ramps, elevators, and other features in most public places. Public transportation, including the subway, buses, and trams, is also equipped with accessibility features such as ramps, designated seating areas, and audio announcements.

However, some older parts of the city, particularly in the Old Town, may have cobblestone streets and narrow passages that could be challenging for wheelchair users.

Stockholm's official visitor website, **Visit Stockholm** (https://www.visitstockholm.com/), provides comprehensive information on accessibility in the city, including details on transportation, accommodations, and attractions. For specific accessibility requirements, it is recommended to contact the respective service providers or attractions directly before your visit.

4. Where to stay in Stockholm

Stockholm is a relatively small city with great transport links and therefore the three-day itinerary included in this book should work regardless of where you choose to stay. Each of the islands that make up Stockholm have their own distinctive feel so here is a short guide to some of the main islands, to help you make up your mind where you would like to stay.

Grand Hotel in Norrmalm

Norrmalm
The area of Norrmalm includes the very centre of the city and is the heart of the action. Here you will find the main shopping streets, the central station and many tourist attractions. There are restaurants and cafés everywhere you look and many different hotels to choose from.

Östermalm
Östermalm, to the east of Norrmalm, is known for being the more luxury part of town. This is where the fashionable people of Stockholm go out to mingle. Here you will find designer shops, exclusive restaurants and high-end hotels. The area is mainly concentrated around Strueplan, where you will find many shops, bars and restaurants.

Södermalm
Södermalm, in the southern part of Stockholm, is more low key than its northern counterparts and is known for its cool, hipster vibe. The island itself is rocky and has many excellent viewpoints overlooking the city. It is also home to shopping streets and many restaurants, cafes and bars.

Södermalm has a much more laid-back feel than Norrmalm or Östermalm, while still being close to all the key tourist attractions.

Gamla Stan
Gamla Stan is the oldest part of Stockholm and walking through its medieval streets really takes you back in time. This is the ultimate Stockholm tourist destination, so if you want to surround yourself in history and really embrace your inner tourist, then Gamla Stan is the place to stay.

AF Chapman hostel moored at Skeppsholmen, Norrmalm

4.1 Best Hotels in Stockholm
If you decide to stay in **Norrmalm**, you should check out the following hotels:

1. Grand Hotel Stockholm: https://booki.ng/2IJPbkb

The Grand Hôtel Stockholm (https://booki.ng/2IJPbkb) is a luxurious and iconic 5-star hotel located in the heart of Stockholm, on the waterfront overlooking the Royal Palace and the Old Town. Established in 1874, the hotel has a rich history and has hosted celebrities, dignitaries, and royalty from around the world.

Accommodations: The Grand Hôtel offers 273 elegantly appointed guest rooms and suites, ranging from stylish Superior Rooms to the lavish Princess Lilian Suite. All rooms feature modern amenities such as complimentary Wi-Fi, flat-screen TVs, minibars, and marble bathrooms. Many rooms boast stunning views of the waterfront and the city's historic skyline.

Dining: The hotel is home to several renowned dining venues, including:

1. The Veranda: A classic Swedish restaurant offering a lavish smörgåsbord, a traditional buffet-style meal featuring an array of hot and cold dishes, as well as à la carte options.
2. Mathias Dahlgren Matbaren: A Michelin-starred restaurant, helmed by acclaimed chef Mathias Dahlgren, offering contemporary Swedish cuisine with a focus on seasonal and locally-sourced ingredients.
3. Cadier Bar: A sophisticated cocktail bar serving expertly crafted drinks and light bites in an elegant setting.

Amenities and Services: Guests at the Grand Hôtel can enjoy an array of world-class amenities and services, such as:

1. Nordic Spa & Fitness: The hotel's on-site spa offers a range of rejuvenating treatments, including massages, facials, and body wraps, as

well as a traditional Swedish sauna, a fitness center, and a heated indoor pool.
2. Conference and Event Facilities: The hotel features 24 versatile meeting and event spaces, including the stunning Spegelsalen ballroom, which can accommodate up to 500 guests for conferences, weddings, or social events.
3. Concierge Service: The hotel's knowledgeable concierge team is available to assist with reservations, transportation, and recommendations for local attractions and experiences.

Location: The Grand Hôtel Stockholm enjoys a prime location, within walking distance of many of the city's top attractions, such as the Royal Palace, the National Museum, and the Vasa Museum. The hotel is also well-connected to public transportation, with the nearest subway station (Kungsträdgården) just a few minutes' walk away.

2. Scandic No 53: https://booki.ng/2rPGZEu

Scandic No 53 (https://booki.ng/2rPGZEu) is a modern and stylish 4-star hotel located in the bustling heart of Stockholm, offering a comfortable and convenient base for both leisure and business travelers. Situated on Kungsgatan, one of Stockholm's main shopping streets, the hotel is within walking distance of many popular attractions, restaurants, and entertainment venues.

Accommodations: Scandic No 53 features 274 contemporary guest rooms, ranging from cozy Economy Rooms to spacious Superior Rooms. All rooms are equipped with essential amenities, such as complimentary Wi-Fi, flat-screen TVs, and comfortable workspaces. The hotel also offers accessible rooms designed to accommodate guests with special needs.

Dining: Guests at Scandic No 53 can enjoy a delicious and varied breakfast buffet featuring a wide selection of hot and cold items, including Swedish classics, fresh fruits, and baked goods. The hotel's on-site restaurant, The Market, serves a menu of international and Swedish dishes made from fresh, locally-sourced ingredients, while the lobby bar offers a relaxed atmosphere for sipping a cocktail or enjoying a light snack.

Amenities and Services: Scandic No 53 provides a range of guest services and amenities to ensure a pleasant stay, such as:

1. Scandic Shop: A 24-hour convenience store located in the hotel lobby, offering snacks, drinks, and travel essentials.
2. Meeting Facilities: The hotel features two flexible meeting rooms, accommodating up to 50 guests for conferences, workshops, or private events.
3. Bicycle Rental: The hotel offers bike rentals, allowing guests to explore the city at their own pace and enjoy Stockholm's extensive network of bike lanes.

Location: Scandic No 53's central location places it within walking distance of numerous attractions, such as the Royal Swedish Opera, Stockholm Central Station, and the Old Town (Gamla Stan). The nearest subway station (Hötorget) is just a short walk away, providing easy access to the rest of the city and its surrounding areas.

3. Lydmar Hotel: http://booki.ng/2Iqs9iX

Lydmar Hotel (http://booki.ng/2Iqs9iX) is a chic and intimate 5-star boutique hotel nestled in the heart of Stockholm, offering a unique and luxurious stay for discerning travelers. With its prime waterfront location, the hotel boasts stunning views of the Royal Palace and the Old Town, while its sophisticated design and attentive service create a welcoming atmosphere.

Accommodations: Lydmar Hotel features 46 individually designed guest rooms and suites, each with its own distinct character and charm. Rooms are spacious and beautifully furnished, with amenities such as complimentary Wi-Fi, flat-screen TVs, minibars, and Nespresso machines. The hotel's rooms and suites are adorned with contemporary art and photography, enhancing the stylish ambiance.

Dining: The hotel's on-site restaurant, Lydmar Dining Room, serves a menu of modern European cuisine, focusing on seasonal and locally-sourced ingredients. The elegant dining room and outdoor terrace offer stunning views of the waterfront, making it a perfect spot for a leisurely meal or a romantic dinner. The hotel's bar and lounge area provide a relaxed setting for enjoying a cocktail or a glass of wine from the extensive list.

Amenities and Services: Lydmar Hotel offers a range of amenities and services to ensure a memorable stay, including:

1. Concierge Service: The hotel's knowledgeable concierge team is available to assist with restaurant reservations, transportation arrangements, and recommendations for local attractions and experiences.
2. Library Lounge: Guests can unwind in the cozy Library Lounge, with its comfortable seating, curated selection of books, and inviting fireplace.
3. Art Exhibitions: The hotel frequently hosts art exhibitions and cultural events, showcasing both local and international artists.

Location: Lydmar Hotel's central location makes it an ideal base for exploring Stockholm's many attractions. The hotel is within walking distance of popular sites such as the National Museum, the Royal Swedish Opera, and Djurgården Island. The nearest subway station (Kungsträdgården) is just a few minutes' walk away, providing convenient access to the rest of the city.

4. Nordic Light Hotel: https://booki.ng/2L7Q2cR

Nordic Light Hotel (https://booki.ng/2L7Q2cR) is a contemporary 4-star hotel situated in the heart of Stockholm, offering a unique blend of Nordic design and hospitality. Its convenient location, just steps away from Stockholm Central Station, makes it an ideal choice for both business and leisure travelers seeking a stylish and comfortable stay.

Accommodations: The hotel features 169 well-appointed guest rooms, ranging from compact Easy Rooms to spacious and luxurious Master Suites. All rooms are designed with a minimalist Nordic aesthetic and include modern amenities such as complimentary Wi-Fi, flat-screen TVs, and air conditioning. Many rooms also offer adjustable mood lighting, allowing guests to create their own personalized ambiance.

Dining: Nordic Light Hotel is home to LYKKE, a modern restaurant that serves a fusion of Nordic and international flavors, focusing on seasonal and locally-sourced ingredients. Guests can also enjoy a daily breakfast buffet featuring a wide variety of hot and cold dishes, including traditional Swedish options. The hotel's bar, LIVINGROOM, offers a relaxed setting for sipping a cocktail or enjoying a light snack.

Amenities and Services: Nordic Light Hotel provides a range of amenities and services designed to enhance guests' stay, such as:

1. Fitness Center: The hotel offers a well-equipped fitness center, featuring a range of cardio and strength training equipment, as well as a relaxation area with a sauna.
2. Meeting and Event Facilities: The hotel features seven versatile meeting rooms, accommodating up to 100 guests for conferences, workshops, or private events.

3. Pet-Friendly: Nordic Light Hotel welcomes pets, providing special amenities and services for furry companions.

Location: The hotel's central location places it within walking distance of many of Stockholm's top attractions, such as the Old Town (Gamla Stan), the Royal Swedish Opera, and the City Hall. Its proximity to Stockholm Central Station provides easy access to the city's public transportation network, including subway, bus, tram, and commuter train connections.

If you decide to stay in **Östermalm**, you should have a look at these hotels:

1. Hotel Drottning Kristina Stureplan: https://booki.ng/2Ioiut3

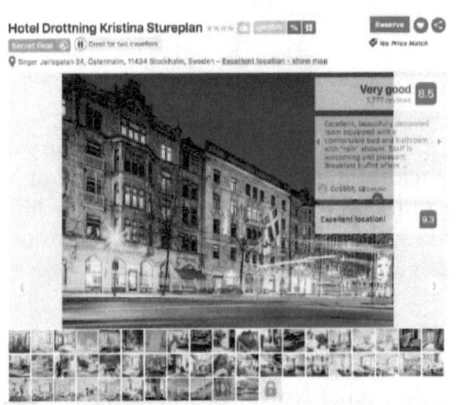

Hotel Drottning Kristina Stureplan (https://booki.ng/2Ioiut3) is an elegant 4-star boutique hotel located in the upscale district of Östermalm in central Stockholm. Housed in a historic 19th-century building, the hotel offers a charming blend of classic design and modern amenities, providing a comfortable and sophisticated stay for guests.

Accommodations: The hotel features 101 tastefully decorated guest rooms, ranging from cozy Standard Rooms to the luxurious Drottning Kristina Suite. All rooms are equipped with essential amenities, such as complimentary Wi-Fi, flat-screen TVs, and minibars. Many rooms also feature high ceilings, large windows, and original architectural details, adding to the hotel's unique charm.

Dining: Hotel Drottning Kristina Stureplan is home to Restaurant TAKO, which offers a fusion of Asian and Scandinavian flavors, focusing on high-quality ingredients and innovative culinary techniques. Guests can also enjoy a daily breakfast buffet, featuring a wide selection of hot and cold items, including traditional Swedish options. The hotel's elegant bar, The Blue Room, provides an intimate setting for sipping a cocktail or enjoying a light snack.

Amenities and Services: Hotel Drottning Kristina Stureplan offers a range of amenities and services designed to enhance guests' stay, such as:

1. Conference and Event Facilities: The hotel features two stylish meeting rooms, accommodating up to 40 guests for conferences, workshops, or private events.
2. Concierge Service: The hotel's knowledgeable concierge team is available to assist with restaurant reservations, transportation arrangements, and recommendations for local attractions and experiences.
3. Courtyard Garden: Guests can relax in the hotel's tranquil courtyard garden, a peaceful oasis in the heart of the city.

Location: The hotel's prime location in Östermalm places it within walking distance of numerous high-end shops, restaurants, and art galleries, as well as popular attractions such as the Royal Dramatic Theatre, the National Museum, and Humlegården Park. The nearest subway station (Östermalmstorg) is just a short walk away, providing convenient access to the rest of the city.

2. Hotel Kung Carl: https://booki.ng/2Iswzln

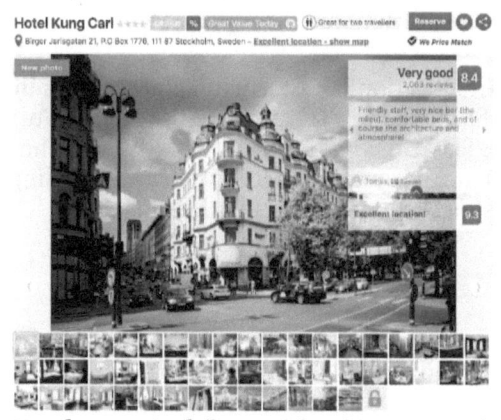

Hotel Kung Carl (https://booki.ng/2Iswzln) is a charming 4-star hotel located in the heart of Stockholm's fashionable Östermalm district. Set within a beautiful 19th-century building, the hotel offers a delightful blend of historic elegance and modern comfort, making it an ideal choice for both leisure and business travelers.

Accommodations: Hotel Kung Carl features 143 individually decorated guest rooms, ranging from cozy Single Rooms to the luxurious Carl Suite. Each room is uniquely designed with a combination of classic and contemporary elements, and comes equipped with amenities such as complimentary Wi-Fi, flat-screen TVs, and minibars. Many rooms also offer stunning views of the surrounding cityscape or the hotel's picturesque courtyard.

Dining: The hotel's on-site restaurant, Kung Carls Bakficka, serves a menu of traditional Swedish and international dishes, made from fresh, locally-sourced ingredients. Guests can also enjoy a daily breakfast buffet, featuring a wide variety of hot and cold items, including Scandinavian classics. The hotel's stylish bar, Bar Kung Carl, offers a selection of expertly crafted cocktails and a relaxed atmosphere, perfect for unwinding after a day of exploring the city.

Amenities and Services: Hotel Kung Carl provides a range of amenities and services to ensure a pleasant stay for its guests, such as:

1. Meeting and Event Facilities: The hotel features five versatile meeting rooms, accommodating up to 100 guests for conferences, workshops, or private events.
2. Fitness Center: Guests have access to a well-equipped fitness center, featuring a range of cardio and strength training equipment.
3. Concierge Service: The hotel's knowledgeable concierge team is available to assist with restaurant reservations, transportation arrangements, and recommendations for local attractions and experiences.

Location: The hotel's central location in Östermalm places it within walking distance of many of Stockholm's top attractions, such as Stureplan Square, the Royal Dramatic Theatre, and the National Museum. The nearest subway station (Östermalmstorg) is just a short walk away, providing convenient access to the rest of the city and its surrounding areas.

If you decide to stay in **Södermalm**, have a look at these hotels:

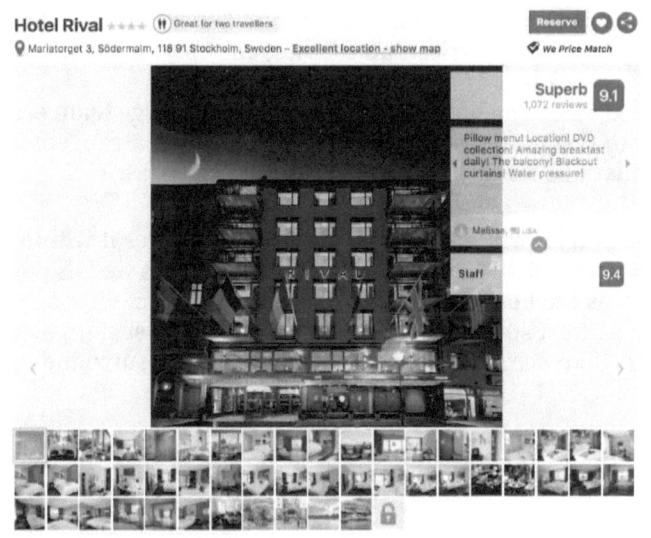

1. Hotel Rival: https://booki.ng/2Iwaxhl

Hotel Rival (https://booki.ng/2Iwaxhl) is a vibrant and stylish 4-star boutique hotel, located in the trendy Södermalm district of Stockholm. Owned by former ABBA member Benny Andersson, the hotel boasts a unique blend of art deco design, modern amenities, and a touch of cinematic glamour, providing a memorable stay for guests seeking a distinctive experience.

Accommodations: Hotel Rival features 99 elegantly designed guest rooms, ranging from cozy Standard Rooms to the luxurious Deluxe Rooms with balconies overlooking the picturesque Mariatorget Square. All rooms are equipped with amenities such as complimentary Wi-Fi, flat-screen TVs, and DVD players, while many also showcase original artwork and unique design features inspired by cinema and music.

Dining: The hotel's on-site restaurant, Bistro Rival, serves a menu of classic Swedish and international dishes, crafted from fresh, locally-sourced ingredients. Guests can enjoy a daily breakfast buffet, featuring a wide variety of hot and cold items, including traditional Swedish options. The hotel's lively bar, Bar Rival, offers an extensive cocktail menu and a relaxed atmosphere, perfect for socializing or enjoying live music and events.

Amenities and Services: Hotel Rival provides a range of amenities and services designed to enhance guests' stay, such as:

1. Cinema and Event Facilities: The hotel features a beautifully restored 1930s cinema, which can be used for movie screenings, conferences, and private events, accommodating up to 700 guests.

2. **Café and Bakery:** The hotel's on-site café and bakery, Rival Café, offers a selection of delicious pastries, sandwiches, and specialty coffee drinks, perfect for a quick bite or a leisurely break.
3. **Concierge Service:** The hotel's knowledgeable concierge team is available to assist with restaurant reservations, transportation arrangements, and recommendations for local attractions and experiences.

Location: The hotel's prime location in Södermalm places it within walking distance of numerous shops, galleries, and restaurants, as well as popular attractions such as the Fotografiska Museum and the Monteliusvägen viewpoint. The nearest subway station (Mariatorget) is just steps away, providing convenient access to the rest of the city and its surrounding areas.

2. Scandic Malmen: https://booki.ng/2GsgASf

Scandic Malmen (https://booki.ng/2GsgASf) is a modern and comfortable 4-star hotel located in the heart of the vibrant Södermalm district in Stockholm. Offering a convenient and enjoyable stay for both leisure and business travelers, the hotel provides easy access to numerous shops, restaurants, and attractions.

Accommodations: Scandic Malmen features 332 well-appointed guest rooms, ranging from cozy Standard Rooms to spacious Superior Rooms with extra amenities. All rooms are designed with a contemporary Scandinavian aesthetic and come equipped with essentials such as complimentary Wi-Fi, flat-screen TVs, and air conditioning. Many rooms also offer stunning views of the surrounding cityscape.

Dining: The hotel's on-site restaurant, Malmen, serves a menu of classic Swedish and international dishes, made from fresh, locally-sourced ingredients. Guests can enjoy a daily breakfast buffet, featuring a wide variety of hot and cold items, including traditional Scandinavian options. The hotel's stylish bar, Bar Malmen, offers a selection of expertly crafted cocktails and a relaxed atmosphere, perfect for unwinding after a day of exploring the city.

Amenities and Services: Scandic Malmen provides a range of amenities and services to ensure a pleasant stay for its guests, such as:
- Fitness Center: Guests have access to a well-equipped fitness center, featuring a range of cardio and strength training equipment, as well as a relaxation area with a sauna.
- Meeting and Event Facilities: The hotel features eight versatile meeting rooms, accommodating up to 150 guests for conferences, workshops, or private events.
- Bicycle Rental: The hotel offers bicycle rentals, allowing guests to explore Stockholm's many attractions and neighborhoods at their own pace.

Location: The hotel's central location in Södermalm places it within walking distance of many of Stockholm's top attractions, such as the Fotografiska Museum, the Monteliusvägen viewpoint, and the trendy SoFo area. The nearest subway station (Medborgarplatsen) is just steps away, providing convenient access to the rest of the city and its surrounding areas.

If you decide to stay in **Gamla Stan,** you should check out these hotels:

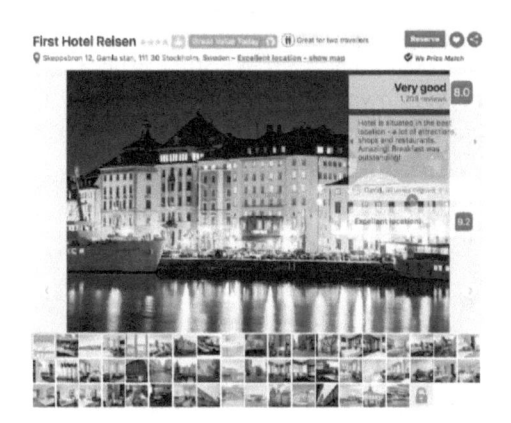

1. First Hotel Reisen: https://booki.ng/2Ipkj9i

First Hotel Reisen (https://booki.ng/2Ipkj9i) is an elegant 4-star hotel located in the historic Old Town (Gamla Stan) of Stockholm. Housed in a beautiful 18th-century building, the hotel offers a unique blend of classic charm and modern amenities, providing a comfortable and memorable stay for guests seeking a taste of Stockholm's rich history.

Accommodations: The hotel features 144 tastefully decorated guest rooms, ranging from cozy Standard Rooms to spacious Deluxe Rooms with waterfront views. All rooms are equipped with essential amenities, such as complimentary Wi-Fi, flat-screen TVs, and minibars. Many rooms also feature high ceilings, large windows, and original architectural details, adding to the hotel's unique charm.

Dining: First Hotel Reisen is home to Reisen Restaurant, which serves a menu of traditional Swedish and international dishes, focusing on high-quality ingredients and innovative culinary techniques. Guests can also enjoy a daily breakfast buffet, featuring a wide selection of hot and cold items, including traditional Swedish options. The hotel's elegant bar, Reisen Bar, provides an intimate setting for sipping a cocktail or enjoying a light snack.

Amenities and Services: First Hotel Reisen offers a range of amenities and services designed to enhance guests' stay, such as:
- Spa and Wellness Facilities: The hotel features a wellness area, offering a range of treatments, a sauna, and a plunge pool for relaxation and rejuvenation.
- Meeting and Event Facilities: The hotel has five versatile meeting rooms, accommodating up to 90 guests for conferences, workshops, or private events.
- Concierge Service: The hotel's knowledgeable concierge team is available to assist with restaurant reservations, transportation arrangements, and recommendations for local attractions and experiences.

Location: The hotel's prime location in Gamla Stan places it within walking distance of numerous historic sites, shops, and restaurants, as well as popular attractions such as the Royal Palace, Stockholm Cathedral, and the Nobel Prize Museum. The nearest subway station (Gamla Stan) is just a short walk away, providing convenient access to the rest of the city and its surrounding areas.

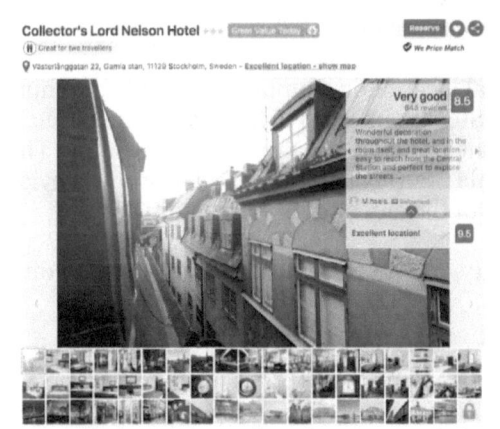

2. Collector's Lord Nelson Hotel: https://booki.ng/2rU1Nea

Collector's Lord Nelson Hotel (https://booki.ng/2rU1Nea) is a charming 3-star boutique hotel located in the heart of Stockholm's historic Old Town (Gamla Stan). Set within a narrow 17th-century building, the hotel offers a distinctive nautical theme and a cozy atmosphere, providing a unique and memorable stay for guests seeking an authentic Swedish experience.

Accommodations: The hotel features 29 individually decorated guest rooms, ranging from compact Single Rooms to spacious Captain's Rooms with private saunas. All rooms are designed with a maritime-inspired aesthetic and come equipped with amenities such as complimentary Wi-Fi, flat-screen TVs, and minibars. Many rooms also offer stunning views of the surrounding Old Town or the hotel's picturesque courtyard.

Dining: Guests at Collector's Lord Nelson Hotel can enjoy a daily breakfast buffet, featuring a wide variety of hot and cold items, including traditional Swedish options. Although the hotel does not have an on-site restaurant, its prime location in Gamla Stan ensures that numerous dining options, ranging from casual cafes to fine dining establishments, are within easy walking distance.

Amenities and Services: Collector's Lord Nelson Hotel provides a range of amenities and services to ensure a pleasant stay for its guests, such as:
1. Rooftop Terrace: Guests can relax on the hotel's rooftop terrace, offering stunning panoramic views of Gamla Stan and the surrounding cityscape.
2. Complimentary Tea and Coffee: The hotel offers complimentary tea and coffee in the lobby throughout the day for guests to enjoy.

3. Concierge Service: The hotel's knowledgeable concierge team is available to assist with restaurant reservations, transportation arrangements, and recommendations for local attractions and experiences.

Location: The hotel's central location in Gamla Stan places it within walking distance of many of Stockholm's top historic attractions, such as the Royal Palace, Stockholm Cathedral, and the Nobel Prize Museum. The nearest subway station (Gamla Stan) is just a short walk away, providing convenient access to the rest of the city and its surrounding areas.

Stockholm is an expensive city, but if you're on a **budget** then try one of these **quirky hostels:**

1. Långholmen Hostel (based in an old prison):

https://booki.ng/2L7uU6k

Långholmen Hostel (https://booki.ng/2L7uU6k) is a unique and affordable accommodation option located on the scenic Långholmen Island in Stockholm. Housed in a former prison building that dates back to the 19th century, the hostel offers guests a distinctive and memorable stay, complete with a fascinating history and a touch of adventure.

Accommodations: The hostel features 94 cozy and comfortable guest rooms, ranging from dormitory-style shared rooms to private cells, retaining the original prison layout. All rooms come with basic amenities such as complimentary Wi-Fi, and shared bathroom facilities. Many rooms also offer stunning views of the surrounding island or the hotel's picturesque courtyard.

Dining: Långholmen Hostel offers a daily breakfast buffet, featuring a wide variety of hot and cold items, including traditional Swedish options. Guests can also make use of the fully-equipped communal kitchen to prepare their meals. The nearby Långholmen Inn, located within the same complex, serves a menu of classic Swedish and international dishes in a relaxed and historic setting.

Amenities and Services: Långholmen Hostel provides a range of amenities and services to ensure a pleasant stay for its guests, such as:
1. Prison Museum: The hostel is home to a small museum that provides an intriguing insight into the building's history as a prison and the lives of its inmates.
2. Bicycle Rental: Guests can rent bicycles from the hostel, allowing them to explore Långholmen Island and the surrounding areas at their own pace.
3. Laundry Facilities: The hostel offers on-site laundry facilities, ensuring guests have access to clean clothes throughout their stay.

Location: The hostel's unique location on Långholmen Island provides guests with a tranquil and picturesque setting, while still offering convenient access to Stockholm's city center. The nearest subway station (Hornstull) is a 10-minute walk away, providing easy access to the rest of the city and its attractions. Långholmen Island itself is home to a beautiful park, beach, and walking paths, offering plenty of opportunities for outdoor activities and relaxation.

2. Af Chapman and Skeppsholmen (a ship from the late 1800s and a former navy barracks): https://booki.ng/2L967yX

Af Chapman and Skeppsholmen (https://booki.ng/2L967yX) offer a truly unique and memorable accommodation experience in Stockholm. The hostel comprises two distinct properties – the Af Chapman, a beautifully restored ship from the late 1800s, and the Skeppsholmen, a former navy barracks – both located on the picturesque Skeppsholmen Island.

Accommodations: The Af Chapman ship features 34 cozy and comfortable guest cabins, ranging from dormitory-style shared rooms to private cabins,

49

all with shared bathroom facilities. The ship retains its original charm and offers stunning views of Stockholm's waterfront and the surrounding cityscape. The Skeppsholmen property offers 45 additional guest rooms, ranging from dormitory-style shared rooms to private en-suite rooms, located in the former navy barracks building.

Dining: Guests at Af Chapman and Skeppsholmen can enjoy a daily breakfast buffet, featuring a wide variety of hot and cold items, including traditional Swedish options. The hostel also offers a fully-equipped communal kitchen, allowing guests to prepare their meals. The nearby island of Skeppsholmen is home to a range of dining options, from casual cafes to fine dining establishments.

Amenities and Services: Af Chapman and Skeppsholmen provide a range of amenities and services to ensure a pleasant stay for their guests, such as:
1. Common Areas: The hostel offers a variety of common areas for relaxation and socializing, including a spacious lounge with comfortable seating and a TV room.
2. Free Wi-Fi: Complimentary Wi-Fi is available throughout the hostel, ensuring guests stay connected during their visit.
3. Laundry Facilities: The hostel offers on-site laundry facilities, providing guests with the convenience of clean clothes throughout their stay.

Location: The hostel's unique location on Skeppsholmen Island provides guests with a tranquil and picturesque setting, while still offering convenient access to Stockholm's city center. The island is home to several museums and attractions, such as the Moderna Museet and the ArkDes architecture and design museum. The nearest bus stop (Skeppsholmen) is just steps away, providing easy access to the rest of the city and its attractions.

3. Rygerfjord Hotel and Hostel (a Norwegian boat from the 1950s): https://booki.ng/2rOUDIo

Rygerfjord Hotel and Hostel (https://booki.ng/2rOUDIo) is a unique and budget-friendly accommodation option in Stockholm, offering guests the opportunity to stay on a historic Norwegian boat from the 1950s. Moored along the picturesque Söder Mälarstrand, the Rygerfjord provides stunning waterfront views and a memorable stay for travelers seeking a truly distinctive experience.

Accommodations: The Rygerfjord features a variety of cozy and comfortable guest cabins, ranging from dormitory-style shared rooms to private cabins, all with shared bathroom facilities. Many cabins offer fantastic views of the surrounding waterfront and cityscape. The rooms are designed with a classic maritime aesthetic, preserving the boat's original charm and character.

Dining: Guests at Rygerfjord Hotel and Hostel can enjoy a daily breakfast buffet, featuring a wide variety of hot and cold items, including traditional Swedish options. The on-board Rygerfjord Restaurant and Bar serves a menu of classic Swedish and international dishes, as well as a selection of beverages, in a relaxed and historic setting with stunning waterfront views.

Amenities and Services: Rygerfjord Hotel and Hostel provides a range of amenities and services to ensure a pleasant stay for its guests, such as:
1. Common Areas: The hostel offers a variety of common areas for relaxation and socializing, including a spacious lounge with comfortable seating, a TV, and board games.
2. Free Wi-Fi: Complimentary Wi-Fi is available throughout the hostel, ensuring guests stay connected during their visit.
3. Luggage Storage: The hostel offers luggage storage facilities for guests who arrive early or wish to explore the city after checking out.

Location: The hostel's unique location along Söder Mälarstrand provides guests with easy access to many of Stockholm's top attractions, such as Gamla Stan, the Royal Palace, and the Vasa Museum. The nearest subway station (Mariatorget) is a 10-minute walk away, providing convenient access to the rest of the city and its surrounding areas.

4. Den Röda Båten ("the red boat" - two red wooden boats with interior décor to match): https://booki.ng/2ItTW24

Den Röda Båten (https://booki.ng/2ItTW24), or "the red boat," is a charming and budget-friendly accommodation option in Stockholm, offering guests the opportunity to stay on one of two red wooden boats with interior décor to match. Moored along the picturesque Söder Mälarstrand, Den Röda Båten provides a cozy and unique atmosphere for travelers seeking a distinctive experience in the heart of Stockholm.

Accommodations:
Den Röda Båten features a variety of cozy and comfortable guest cabins, ranging from dormitory-style shared rooms to private cabins with en-suite bathrooms. The rooms are designed with a classic maritime aesthetic, preserving the boats' original charm and character. Many cabins offer fantastic views of the surrounding waterfront and cityscape.

Dining:
Guests at Den Röda Båten can enjoy a daily breakfast buffet, featuring a wide variety of hot and cold items, including traditional Swedish options. The on-board café and bar serve a selection of beverages, light snacks, and sandwiches, providing a relaxed setting for guests to unwind after a day of exploring the city.

Amenities and Services:
Den Röda Båten provides a range of amenities and services to ensure a pleasant stay for its guests, such as:

- Common Areas: The hostel offers a variety of common areas for relaxation and socializing, including a spacious lounge with comfortable seating, a TV, and board games.

- Free Wi-Fi: Complimentary Wi-Fi is available throughout the hostel, ensuring guests stay connected during their visit.
- Luggage Storage: The hostel offers luggage storage facilities for guests who arrive early or wish to explore the city after checking out.

Location:

The hostel's unique location along Söder Mälarstrand provides guests with easy access to many of Stockholm's top attractions, such as Gamla Stan, the Royal Palace, and the Vasa Museum. The nearest subway station (Mariatorget) is a 10-minute walk away, providing convenient access to the rest of the city and its surrounding areas.

5. Dining and Cuisine
5.1. Traditional Swedish Foods

This is a section in our guide for the food lovers, explaining how to make the most of your culinary experience in Sweden, with a list of the must-try dishes in Stockholm.

Swedish cuisine is typically salty and vinegary due to the country's history of having to preserve food through the long winters, so it might take a little getting used to if you don't usually eat a lot of salt. However, once you've got over the food seeming perhaps a little strange, you will find a lot of great Swedish food in Stockholm.

Fika
One of the most important parts of Swedish culture is fika, which is essentially a coffee and cake break. No trip to Sweden would be complete without many fika breaks, meaning you should have plenty of opportunities to try all of these different types of fika:

Cinnamon buns (kanelbullar) are perhaps the most famous of all Swedish baked goods. These are a popular part of fika and can be found all year round and in pretty much any bakery or shop you go to. There is even a special day dedicated to cinnamon buns, celebrated on October 4th every year.

Cinamon buns (kanelbullar)

If you are not a fan of cinnamon, you can try their cardamom counterparts (kardemummabullar), which are arguably even more delicious.

In February, Swedes celebrate Shrove Tuesday with cream buns (semlor). These are large buns flavoured with cardamom and filled with almond paste and whipped cream. They can even be enjoyed in a bowl of warm milk.

Cream bun (semla)

At Christmas it's time for saffron buns (lussekatter or lussebullar). A little less sweet than a traditional cake, but still an excellent fika choice, these buns are flavoured with saffron and raisins and can be enjoyed with a nice glass of glögg (Swedish mulled wine).

Saffron buns (lussekatter)

In between fika, you're probably going to want to eat some more savoury food, so here is a list of some tasty traditional Swedish dishes not to be missed:

Surströmming
When talking about Swedish food, most people will likely mention the infamous fermented herring that smells so bad you have to eat it outdoors. Contrary to popular belief amongst foreigners, this is not commonly eaten and most Stockholmers have probably not even tried it themselves, or maybe just once as a dare. If you can find some and you're feeling brave, by all means give it a go, but make sure you wash it down with a shot of aquavit (a traditional Scandinavian spirit, distilled from grain or potatoes) as is tradition.

Meatballs
Köttbullar, as they are known in Swedish, are probably one of the most famous elements of Swedish cuisine, probably partly thanks to Ikea restaurants. To enjoy them properly they should be served with mashed potato, lingon berries and a creamy gravy.

Västerbotten pie

This pie, made with Västerbotten cheese from the north of Sweden, is a popular Swedish food and can be served with a variety of side dishes, or enjoyed on its own.

Gravad lax
Salmon cured in salt, sugar and dill (gravad lax) is a classic Nordic dish and is usually served as a starter, sliced very finely. If you're unsure about all this fermented fish but want to get a taste of some real traditional Nordic food, then gravad lax is a great option.

Smörgåstårta
Literally translated as "sandwich cake", smörgåstårta is exactly that, a sandwich put together like a cake. It is commonly eaten at parties and similar events but can also be found at cafes and is a great lunch option. It is usually constructed from several layers of bread and has creamy fillings in between, typically involving mayonnaise. Although there are many different fillings which can be used, smörgåstårta usually includes things such as prawns, ham, tomatoes, cucumber, paté, smoked salmon and grapes.

Smörgåstorta (translates as "sandwich cake")

Crayfish
In August, Swedes hold crayfish parties, where they get together, eat crayfish, drink snaps (shots of alcohol) and sing traditional drinking songs. The crayfish are boiled in salt water and seasoned with dill. They are usually served along with other traditional Swedish foods, such as Västerbotten pie, in a large buffet.

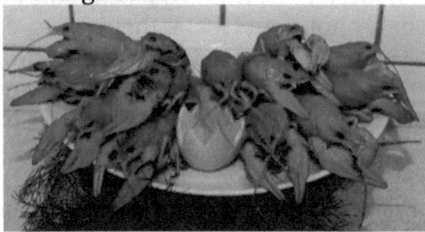

Crayfish served with lemon and dill

Julbord

At Christmas it is traditional to have a Christmas buffet (julbord), which includes many traditional Swedish foods such as meatballs, pickled herring, white fish, ham, sausages and rye bread, amongst much more. For anyone wanting to try as much Swedish food as possible, the julbord is perfect. In December, many restaurants in Stockholm serve julbords, so if you're visiting at this time of year, don't miss out on the opportunity.

5.2. Recommended Restaurants

1. **Tradition** (http://www.restauranttradition.se/)
Located in the heart of Gamla Stan, Tradition offers classic Swedish cuisine in a cozy and authentic setting. With dishes such as herring, gravlax, and Swedish meatballs on the menu, you can experience true Swedish flavors. Price range: SEK 120-250 per main course

2. **Smorgastarteriet** (https://www.smorgastarteriet.se/)
This modern Nordic restaurant in Södermalm offers a seasonal menu that showcases local and sustainable ingredients. Their tasting menu is highly recommended for a full dining experience. Price range: SEK 795 for the tasting menu

3. **Pelikan** (http://www.pelikan.se/)
Pelikan is a historic beer hall in Södermalm that serves traditional Swedish dishes in a lively atmosphere. Enjoy favorites like herring, cured salmon, and venison, accompanied by a great selection of beer. Price range: SEK 100-300 per main course

4. **Oaxen Slip** (https://oaxen.com/slip/)
Located on Djurgården Island, Oaxen Slip is a Nordic bistro that offers delicious dishes made from locally-sourced ingredients. With a focus on sustainability, the restaurant is set in a beautifully restored shipyard building. Price range: SEK 165-395 per main course

5.3. Vegetarian and Vegan Options

1. **Hermans** (https://hermans.se/)
Hermans is a popular vegetarian and vegan restaurant in Södermalm that offers an all-you-can-eat buffet with a wide range of international dishes. Enjoy stunning views of the city from their terrace. Price range: SEK 215 for the buffet (weekdays), SEK 235 (weekends)

2. **Vete-Katten** (https://www.vetekatten.se/)
This historic pastry shop and café in Norrmalm offers a variety of vegetarian sandwiches, salads, and traditional Swedish pastries. It's an excellent spot for fika or a light lunch. Price range: SEK 50-150 per dish

3. **Mahalo** (http://mahalo.se/)

Mahalo is a vegan café and health food restaurant in Vasastan, offering a range of smoothie bowls, salads, wraps, and raw desserts. The vibrant atmosphere and delicious food make it a popular choice for health-conscious diners. Price range: SEK 95-150 per dish

4. **Chutney** (http://www.chutney.se/)
Located in Södermalm, Chutney is a cozy vegetarian and vegan restaurant serving a variety of international dishes, such as Indian curries, Middle Eastern mezze, and Italian pasta. The menu changes daily, ensuring fresh and seasonal options. Price range: SEK 115-145 per main course

5.4. Cafes and Coffee Shops
1. **Fika** (http://www.fikastockholm.se/)
With multiple locations across the city, Fika is a trendy and popular café chain offering high-quality coffee, pastries, and light meals in a cozy and stylish setting. It's an ideal spot for a quick break or to catch up with friends.

2. **Kaffebar** (https://www.kaffebar.se/)
Located in Södermalm, Kaffebar is a small and charming café offering expertly brewed coffee, tasty sandwiches, and delicious pastries. The café's friendly atmosphere and laid-back vibe make it a favorite among locals.

3. **Drop Coffee** (https://www.dropcoffee.se/)
This specialty coffee shop in Vasastan roasts their own beans and offers a selection of high-quality, single-origin coffees. Enjoy your coffee with a variety of pastries and cakes, or attend one of their coffee tastings to learn more about the world of coffee.

4. **Vete-Katten** (https://www.vetekatten.se/)
A historic café and pastry shop in Norrmalm, Vete-Katten is a must-visit for anyone seeking a taste of traditional Swedish fika. With a wide range of pastries, cakes, and sandwiches, the café offers a unique and charming atmosphere that transports you back in time.

5.5. Swedish Fika Culture

Fika is an essential aspect of Swedish culture and daily life. It's more than just a coffee break; it's a time to slow down, socialize, and enjoy life's small pleasures. Traditionally, fika consists of coffee or tea, often accompanied by a sweet treat like a cinnamon bun or a slice of cake. The ritual of fika is deeply ingrained in Swedish society and can be enjoyed at any time of the day, either alone or with friends, family, or colleagues.
While in Stockholm, be sure to embrace the fika culture by visiting local cafes and coffee shops. Take a break from sightseeing or shopping to sit down, relax, and savor a cup of coffee and a delicious pastry. Fika is not just

about the food and drink; it's about the experience and the opportunity to connect with others and yourself.

6. Culture and Entertainment in Stockholm

Stockholm is a city with a rich and vibrant cultural scene, offering a diverse array of entertainment options for visitors and locals alike. From museums and galleries to theaters and music venues, Stockholm has something to offer for everyone who appreciates art, culture, and entertainment. The city is home to some of the world's most impressive museums, including the Nationalmuseum and the Moderna Museet, which showcase the best of Swedish and international art and design.

Stockholm also has a thriving performing arts scene, with numerous theaters and concert halls hosting a wide range of performances throughout the year, from opera and ballet to contemporary dance and experimental theater. In addition, Stockholm is known for its vibrant music scene, with everything from indie rock and electronic music to jazz and classical music being celebrated in the city's many clubs and venues.

Whether you're interested in history, art, or entertainment, Stockholm has something to offer for everyone, making it a truly unique and dynamic cultural destination. In this section, we'll explore some of the best cultural and entertainment options that Stockholm has to offer, highlighting the must-see attractions and events that every visitor should experience during their time in this remarkable city.

6.1 Art Galleries

Stockholm is home to a thriving art scene, with numerous galleries and museums showcasing the best of Swedish and international art and design. Here are some of the top art galleries in Stockholm that you won't want to miss:

1. Nationalmuseum

The Nationalmuseum is Sweden's largest art museum, featuring a collection of over 700,000 works of art from the Middle Ages to the 20th century. The museum's impressive collection includes paintings, sculptures, and decorative arts from around the world, and is known for its outstanding collection of Swedish art. The museum's highlights include works by famous artists such as Rembrandt, Rubens, and Goya, as well as Swedish masters such as Anders Zorn and Carl Larsson.

Visitor Information:
- Opening Hours: Open Tuesday to Sunday from 11:00am to 5:00pm, with extended hours on Thursdays until 8:00pm.
- Ticket Price: Admission is free for the permanent collection, but some special exhibits may charge an admission fee.
- Website: https://www.nationalmuseum.se/en/visit

2. Moderna Museet

Moderna Museet is one of Scandinavia's leading museums of modern and contemporary art. The museum features a diverse collection of works from the 20th century to the present day, including pieces by famous artists such as Pablo Picasso, Salvador Dali, and Andy Warhol. The museum also hosts temporary exhibitions, as well as screenings and other events.

Visitor Information:
- Opening Hours: Open Tuesday to Sunday from 10:00am to 6:00pm, with extended hours on Thursdays until 8:00pm.
- Ticket Price: Admission is free for the permanent collection, but some special exhibits may charge an admission fee.
- Website: https://www.modernamuseet.se/stockholm/en/

3. Fotografiska Stockholm

Fotografiska Stockholm is a contemporary photography museum that showcases both Swedish and international photographers. The museum features rotating exhibits, workshops, and events, as well as a café and restaurant with stunning waterfront views. The museum's highlights include works by famous photographers such as Annie Leibovitz, Robert Mapplethorpe, and David LaChapelle.

Visitor Information:
- Opening Hours: Open Monday to Sunday from 9:00am to 11:00pm, with varying hours for the exhibitions.
- Ticket Price: 170 SEK (approximately $20 USD) for adults, free for children under 12.
- Website: https://www.fotografiska.com/sto/en/

4. Magasin III Museum & Foundation for Contemporary Art

Magasin III is a contemporary art museum that focuses on works by emerging and mid-career artists from around the world. The museum's collection includes works in a variety of media, including painting, sculpture, installation, and video. The museum also hosts temporary exhibitions, as well as artist talks and other events.

Visitor Information:
- Opening Hours: Open Thursday to Sunday from 12:00pm to 6:00pm, with extended hours on Thursdays until 8:00pm.
- Ticket Price: Admission is free for the permanent collection, but some special exhibits may charge an admission fee.
- Website: https://www.magasin3.com/en/

5. Bonniers Konsthall

Bonniers Konsthall is a contemporary art museum that showcases works by both established and emerging artists from around the world. The museum's collection includes works in a variety of media, including painting, sculpture, installation, and video. The museum also hosts temporary exhibitions, as well as artist talks and other events.

Visitor Information:
- Opening Hours: Open Tuesday to Sunday from 12:00pm to 6:00pm
- Ticket Price: Admission is free for the permanent collection, but some special exhibits may charge an admission fee.
- Website: https://www.bonnierskonsthall.se/en/

Tips for Visitors:
1. Check for special exhibitions and events before you go. Many of the galleries in Stockholm host temporary exhibits, artist talks, and other events throughout the year, so be sure to check their websites or social media accounts before you visit to see what's on.
2. Consider purchasing a Stockholm Pass. This pass gives you free admission to many of the top attractions in the city, including some of the art galleries listed above, and can save you money if you plan on visiting several attractions during your stay.
3. Take advantage of the guided tours. Many of the art galleries in Stockholm offer guided tours of their exhibits, which can be a great way to learn more about the artwork and the artists behind it. Check with the gallery or museum to see if they offer any guided tours during your visit.
4. Plan your visit for a weekday if possible. Some of the art galleries in Stockholm can be quite busy on weekends, so if you're able to visit during the week, you may be able to avoid the crowds and have a more enjoyable experience.
5. Don't forget to take breaks. Visiting art galleries can be tiring, so be sure to take breaks and rest your feet if needed. Many of the galleries have cafes or restaurants where you can grab a snack or a drink, or you can take a break outside and enjoy the beautiful views of Stockholm's waterfront.

6.2 Theaters and Performing Arts

Stockholm is home to a vibrant performing arts scene, with numerous theaters and concert halls hosting a wide range of performances throughout the year. Here are some of the top theaters and performing arts venues in Stockholm that you won't want to miss:

1. The Royal Swedish Opera

The Royal Swedish Opera, or Kungliga Operan, is one of the most prestigious opera houses in the world. The venue hosts a variety of operas, ballets, and other performances, featuring both Swedish and international artists. The building itself is a stunning example of neoclassical architecture and is located in the heart of Stockholm.

Visitor Information:

- Opening Hours: Varies depending on the performance.
- Ticket Price: Varies depending on the performance.
- Website: https://www.operan.se/en/

2. Dramaten - The Royal Dramatic Theatre

Dramaten, or The Royal Dramatic Theatre, is Sweden's national theater and is renowned for its high-quality productions of classical and contemporary plays. The theater's repertoire includes works by both Swedish and international playwrights, and the venue is located in a historic building in the heart of Stockholm.

Visitor Information:
- Opening Hours: Varies depending on the performance.
- Ticket Price: Varies depending on the performance.
- Website: https://www.dramaten.se/en/

3. Cirkus

Cirkus is a unique venue that hosts a variety of circus and variety shows, as well as concerts and other events. The venue is housed in a circular building that dates back to the early 20th century and features stunning Art Nouveau architecture. Cirkus is located in the popular Djurgården area of Stockholm, which is home to several other popular tourist attractions.

Visitor Information:
- Opening Hours: Varies depending on the performance.
- Ticket Price: Varies depending on the performance.
- Website: https://www.cirkus.se/en/

4. Stockholm Concert Hall

The Stockholm Concert Hall, or Konserthuset, is one of the most important concert halls in Sweden and is known for its exceptional acoustics. The venue hosts a variety of classical and contemporary concerts, featuring both Swedish and international musicians. The building itself is an iconic example of functionalist architecture and is located in the heart of Stockholm.

Visitor Information:
- Opening Hours: Varies depending on the performance.
- Ticket Price: Varies depending on the performance.
- Website: https://www.konserthuset.se/en/

5. Södra Teatern

Södra Teatern is a popular theater and concert venue that hosts a wide range of events, from theater productions and dance performances to concerts and club nights. The venue is housed in a historic building in the trendy Södermalm neighborhood of Stockholm and features stunning views of the city.

Visitor Information:
- Opening Hours: Varies depending on the performance.
- Ticket Price: Varies depending on the performance.
- Website: https://sodrateatern.com/en/

Tips for Visitors:
1. Check for matinee performances. Many of the theaters in Stockholm offer matinee performances during the day, which can be a great way to experience a performance at a lower cost.
2. Dress appropriately. Many of the theaters in Stockholm have dress codes, so be sure to check with the venue before you go to ensure that you're dressed appropriately.
3. Book your tickets in advance. Some of the most popular performances in Stockholm sell out quickly, so be sure to book your tickets well in advance if possible.
4. Consider attending a concert or show at a smaller venue. Stockholm is home to a number of smaller theaters and concert halls that offer a more intimate and immersive experience.
5. Take advantage of the surrounding area. Many of the theaters and performing arts venues in Stockholm are located in some of the city's most popular neighborhoods, so be sure to explore the area before or after your performance. For example, the Royal Swedish Opera is located in the Gamla Stan neighborhood, which is known for its historic architecture and charming cobblestone streets, while Södra Teatern is located in the trendy Södermalm neighborhood, which is known for its hip cafes, bars, and shops.
6. Check for student discounts. Many of the theaters and performing arts venues in Stockholm offer discounts for students, so be sure to bring your student ID with you if you have one.
7. Don't be afraid to ask for recommendations. The staff at the theaters and performing arts venues in Stockholm are often very knowledgeable about the local arts scene and can provide valuable recommendations and insights into the best performances to see during your visit.

6.3 Nightlife in Stockholm

Stockholm is a city with a thriving nightlife scene, offering visitors a wide range of options for a night out on the town. From trendy bars and clubs to live music venues and comedy clubs, Stockholm has something to offer for everyone. Here are some of the top nightlife destinations in Stockholm:

1. Stureplan

Stureplan is one of the most popular nightlife destinations in Stockholm, known for its trendy bars and clubs. The area is home to several popular nightclubs, such as Sturecompagniet and Café Opera, as well as upscale bars and restaurants. Stureplan is a great place to see and be seen, and is popular with both locals and visitors alike.

Visitor Information:
- Location: Stureplan, Östermalm
- Opening Hours: Varies depending on the venue.
- Website: https://www.stureplan.se/en/

2. Södermalm

Södermalm is a trendy neighborhood in Stockholm that is known for its vibrant nightlife scene. The area is home to a variety of bars, clubs, and music venues, as well as alternative comedy clubs and theaters. Some of the most popular venues include Debaser, Marie Laveau, and Hornstull Strand.

Visitor Information:
- : Södermalm
- Opening Hours: Varies depending on the venue.
- Website: https://www.visitstockholm.com/see--do/attractions/nightlife/

3. Mosebacke Etablissement

Mosebacke Etablissement is a popular venue located in the heart of Södermalm that hosts a variety of events, from live music and comedy shows to theater and dance performances. The venue has a cozy atmosphere and a rooftop terrace with stunning views of Stockholm's skyline.

Visitor Information:
- Location: Mosebacke Torg 1-3, Södermalm
- Opening Hours: Varies depending on the event.
- Website: https://mosebacketerrassen.se/en/

4. Berns

Berns is a historic entertainment venue that dates back to the late 19th century. The venue hosts a variety of events, including live music, theater, and comedy shows, as well as club nights and dance parties. Berns is known for its stunning Art Nouveau architecture and is a popular destination for both locals and visitors.

Visitor Information:
- Location: Berzelii Park, Norrmalm
- Opening Hours: Varies depending on the event.
- Website: https://www.berns.se/en/

5. Mälarpaviljongen

Mälarpaviljongen is a popular outdoor bar and restaurant located on the waterfront in the Kungsholmen neighborhood of Stockholm. The venue features a large outdoor terrace with stunning views of the water and is a great place to relax with a drink and watch the sunset.

Visitor Information:
- Location: Norr Mälarstrand 64, Kungsholmen
- Opening Hours: Open daily from 11:00am to 1:00am.
- Website: https://www.malarpaviljongen.se/en/

Tips for Visitors:
1. Dress to impress. Many of the nightclubs and upscale bars in Stockholm have dress codes, so be sure to dress appropriately if you plan on visiting these venues.
2. Plan ahead. Some of the most popular venues in Stockholm can get crowded, especially on weekends, so be sure to plan ahead and arrive early if possible.
3. Check for special events. Many of the bars and clubs in Stockholm host special events and theme nights throughout the week, so be sure to check their websites or social media accounts to see what's on.
4. Stay safe. As with any big city, it's important to stay safe when enjoying Stockholm's nightlife. Be aware of your surroundings, avoid walking alone at night, and keep an eye on your belongings at all times.
5. Use public transportation. Stockholm's public transportation system is safe and efficient, and is a great way to get around the city at night. Consider taking the subway or a bus to your destination, or use a taxi service like Uber or Lyft.
6. Try some local specialties. Stockholm is known for its craft cocktails, and many of the city's bars and clubs feature unique and inventive drinks. Be sure to try some local specialties, such as a lingonberry-infused cocktail or a traditional Swedish snaps.
7. Explore different neighborhoods. Stockholm has a variety of neighborhoods, each with its own unique character and nightlife scene. Don't be afraid to explore different parts of the city and try out different venues to find your perfect night out.
8. Be prepared for the price. Stockholm can be an expensive city, and this is especially true when it comes to nightlife. Be prepared to pay a premium for drinks and cover charges at some of the city's most popular venues.

Overall, Stockholm's nightlife scene is diverse and exciting, with something to offer for everyone. Whether you're looking for a trendy nightclub, a cozy bar, or a live music venue, Stockholm has plenty of options to choose from. Just be sure to plan ahead, stay safe, and have fun!

6.4 Shopping in Stockholm

Stockholm is a great destination for shoppers, offering a wide range of stores and boutiques to suit every taste and budget. From high-end fashion and designer labels to vintage and secondhand shops, there's something for everyone in Stockholm. Here are some of the top shopping destinations in the city:

1. Drottninggatan

Drottninggatan is one of Stockholm's main shopping streets, lined with a variety of shops and department stores. The street stretches from Gamla Stan to the north, and is home to popular retailers such as H&M, Zara, and Lindex.

Visitor Information:

- Location: Drottninggatan, Norrmalm
- Opening Hours: Varies depending on the store.
- Website: https://www.visitstockholm.com/see--do/attractions/shopping/

2. Mall of Scandinavia

Mall of Scandinavia is one of the largest shopping centers in Scandinavia, featuring over 200 stores and restaurants. The mall is located in the Solna neighborhood, just north of Stockholm, and is easily accessible by public transportation.

Visitor Information:

- Location: Råsta Strandväg 19A, Solna
- Opening Hours: Open daily from 10:00am to 9:00pm.
- Website: https://mallofscandinavia.se/en/

3. Gamla Stan

Gamla Stan, or the Old Town, is a historic neighborhood in the heart of Stockholm that is known for its charming cobblestone streets and quaint shops. The area is home to a variety of boutiques and souvenir shops, selling everything from Swedish handicrafts to designer jewelry.

Visitor Information:

- Location: Gamla Stan, Stockholm
- Opening Hours: Varies depending on the store.
- Website: https://www.visitstockholm.com/see--do/attractions/shopping/

4. NK

NK, or Nordiska Kompaniet, is one of Stockholm's most prestigious department stores, featuring a variety of high-end fashion brands and designer labels. The store is located in the Norrmalm neighborhood and is known for its luxurious atmosphere and exceptional customer service.

Visitor Information:

- Location: Hamngatan 18-20, Norrmalm
- Opening Hours: Open daily from 10:00am to 8:00pm.
- Website: https://www.nk.se/en/

5. Södermalm

Södermalm is a trendy neighborhood in Stockholm that is known for its alternative fashion and vintage shops. The area is home to a variety of boutiques and secondhand stores, selling everything from retro clothing to vinyl records.

Visitor Information:

- Location: Södermalm, Stockholm
- Opening Hours: Varies depending on the store.
- Website: https://www.visitstockholm.com/see--do/attractions/shopping/

Tips for Visitors:

1. Look for tax-free shopping. Many stores in Stockholm offer tax-free shopping for visitors from outside the EU, which can save you money on your purchases. Be sure to ask about tax-free shopping before making your purchase.
2. Visit during sales season. Like many European cities, Stockholm has sales seasons twice a year, typically in January and July. This can be a great time to find discounts on your favorite brands and designers.
3. Explore different neighborhoods. Stockholm has a variety of neighborhoods, each with its own unique shopping scene. Be sure to explore different parts of the city and try out different shops and boutiques to find your perfect style.
4. Be prepared for the price. Stockholm can be an expensive city, and this is especially true when it comes to shopping. Be prepared to pay a premium for designer labels and high-end fashion.

7. Seasonal activities in Stockholm

The three-day itinerary in this guide is designed so it can be used regardless of what time of year you visit Stockholm. However, as seasons vary so greatly in this northern city, there are many fun things you can only do at certain times of year. Here are some great seasonal options you can squeeze into your trip.

7.1 Summer

Most Swedes would argue that summer is the best time to visit Stockholm, with its long, bright days and sunshine. From April onward, restaurants open their outdoor serving and Swedes seek out any patch of sun they can find. Not a moment is to be spent indoors until September. With that in mind, here are some activities that are great for the summer:

#1 Stockholm City Hall: https://international.stockholm.se/the-city-hall/

Stockholm City Hall (Stadshuset) is a council office, ceremonial hall, art gallery, restaurant and major tourist attraction all rolled into one. Of course you can (and should) visit the City Hall whatever time of the year you come to Stockholm, however spring/summer is the best time for two reasons. Firstly, between March and August you can take a guided tour of the building in English (tours in Swedish are available all year round). As the City Hall is a political office building, a guided tour is the only way to get inside. The tour takes around 45 minutes and includes the impressive Blue and Golden Halls, known for hosting the Nobel Banquet and ball respectively, following the annual prize giving ceremonies. Secondly, as well as getting inside the building, during May to September you can climb the 106-metre high tower and enjoy stunning views over the whole of Stockholm, including a perfect aerial view of Gamla Stan. As with the City Hall itself, it is not possible to climb the tower alone, so you need to buy a ticket and book a tour; tickets for the tower are separate to the City Hall tour tickets.

Even if you don't go inside the City Hall, the small grounds surrounding the building are nice to visit. The building stands by the edge of the water, across from which you can see Gamla Stan, the iconic spire of Riddarholmen church, the rocky hills of Södermalm and the Djurgården ferry, shuttling people back and forth across the lake. It's a beautiful place to relax for a while and get some memorable souvenir photos.

City Hall tour tickets cost up to SEK 110.
Tours start at 10 am and run every 30-60 minutes depending on the month. The last tour is usually around 3-4 pm.
Tickets to go up the tower cost SEK 50.
Tours run every 40 minutes from 9.10 am until 3.50 pm, or 5.10 pm in June, July and August.
It is not possible to book tickets for the City Hall or the tower in advance. You need to go to the ticket office on the day you wish to take the tour.

#2 **Gröna Lund:** https://www.gronalund.com/en/

Gröna Lund is Sweden's oldest amusement park and is not without the expected roller coasters, tunnel of love and haunted house. There are also plenty of games where you can win oversized bars of chocolate; something you won't feel you need until you see everyone else walking around with theirs.

While Gröna Lund is great fun for those who love theme parks, what makes it extra special is its annual line up of concerts, including artists who range from popular Swedish musicians to international superstars such as Elton John. This makes Gröna Lund a strong summer favourite among locals. Arrive early in the evening if you want to see a popular band as it's likely the rest of Stockholm will want to do the same.

Gröna Lund is open from May to August, with selected days in September. Entrance before 6 pm costs SEK 120, which gives you access to the park including any concerts that day. Ride tickets must be purchased in addition to the entrance fee.
More detailed ticket information can be found here:
https://www.gronalund.com/en/Plan-Your-Visit/Prices-tickets/
Tickets can be bought online or at the Gröna Lund ticket office.

#3 **Kayaking:** https://langholmenkajak.se/en
With so much water surrounding the entire city it makes sense that water activities are a big part of life in Stockholm. If you fancy more than just swimming and boat trips then from around May to September you can rent a

kayak and paddle through lake Mälaren, regardless of whether you have previous experience or if it's your very first time.

Beginners can go on a guided tour, you can even take a two-man kayak if you're uneasy about going it alone or would just enjoy the company. As well as teaching you how to kayak, the tour guide will give you some of the history of Stockholm as you paddle round. There are different length tours available depending on how much time you have to spend.

For those who are more confident in a kayak, you can rent one and go out as you wish. There's no need to worry about getting lost as there are several recommended routes you can follow if you're unsure of your way around.

If you're feeling more adventurous you can also rent stand-up paddle boards and why not try out stand-up paddle board yoga while you're there?

Guided tours can cost around SEK 500-700 depending on the length.
A one-man kayak costs SEK 250 to rent for two hours, including life jacket, paddle, dry bag and a map.

For those who are enthusiastic about kayaking and have a little more time to spare, it is also possible to escape the city and take a kayaking trip out in the archipelago where you can go island hopping and enjoy the nature. More information about various tour options can be found here:
http://www.truenaturesweden.com/kayak-archipelago/

7.2 Winter

Particularly for visitors from destinations farther south, Stockholm in winter can be a totally different and magical experience. From December, every window is lit up with advent lamps, fairy lights line every balcony and shops place candles outside the doorway to welcome in visitors. While there may not be much daylight, it certainly isn't dark. In addition, there are still plenty of fun things to do. Here are some excellent winter activities:

#1 Ice skating

There are many skating rinks in Stockholm, but arguably the most interesting one is at Kungsträdgården. This outdoor rink set up around a statue in the middle of the park, is popular among both locals and tourists. There is music playing and small wooden huts where you can rent skates or buy coffee; you can even cook your own hot dog over an open fire. The rink is open from November until March, it's free to use but you need to pay to hire skates.

If that all sounds too urban for you, then once the water surrounding the city has frozen over (usually by January or February) you can venture out and explore on skates. Unless you're experienced at skating on natural ice then you should [book a tour](#) as it can be dangerous for those who don't know what they're doing. Tour guides are knowledgeable about the local ice conditions and also have all the appropriate safety equipment and training. An introduction tour takes 5 to 6 hours and costs SEK 1590 for an adult.

#2 Skiing

While Stockholm may not be known for its skiing and there are certainly no mountains, that doesn't stop the ski-loving Swedes. For traditional down-hill skiing, [Hammarbybacken](#) has several slopes and you can also rent gear. It's easily reached by public transport from central Stockholm and is both beginner friendly as well as great fun for those with more experience.

For a more Nordic experience, just 15 minutes outside of the city centre, you can try cross country skiing at [Hellasgården](#). There are several different cross-country tracks to have a go at and afterwards you can enjoy a sauna and a dip in the icy lake. There are also many other activities to do at Hellasgården so it's a great place for a day trip.

Adult ski-rental equipment costs SEK 190 for an hour and a half, or SEK 550 for the day. It can get pretty busy at the weekend, so plan your trip for a week day if you can.

#3 Christmas markets

December is an excellent time to visit Stockholm for the festive vibe. Keep an eye out for the uniquely Scandinavian Christmas décor such as straw goats and gnomes, or head to a Christmas market to get your own. There are a couple of really nice Christmas markets to visit in Stockholm. The first is in the main square (Stortorget) in the old town (Gamla Stan). It may be quite small but the market, with wooden stalls circling round the cobbled square, surrounded by medieval buildings, is like something out of a story book.

The second popular Christmas market is at open-air museum Skansen. They too have the market set up in the town square, but as well as the stalls, here you will also found other festivities, such as music and dancing around the large Christmas tree.

Christmas markets are usually open from the beginning of December and run up until Christmas (celebrated on December 24).

8. Day Trips and Excursions

Stockholm is a beautiful city filled with history, culture, and stunning architecture. However, the surrounding areas also have much to offer, with a wealth of scenic and historic sites just a short journey away. Taking a day trip or excursion is an excellent way to experience the diverse landscapes and rich heritage of Sweden. In this section, we will explore two popular day trips from Stockholm: Archipelago Cruises and a visit to Sigtuna, Sweden's oldest town.

8.1. Archipelago Cruises

The Stockholm Archipelago is a breathtaking collection of over 30,000 islands, islets, and rocks scattered along the coastline of the Baltic Sea. Taking an archipelago cruise is a fantastic way to explore this stunning natural wonder and experience the beauty of Sweden's coastal landscapes.

Several companies offer archipelago cruises, ranging from short excursions to full-day trips. One popular option is Stromma (https://www.stromma.com/en-se/stockholm/excursions/), which offers a variety of guided tours and hop-on-hop-off boat services.

Cruises typically depart from Stockholm's city center and take you through the picturesque waterways, with stops at charming islands and towns along the way.

Some popular destinations include Vaxholm, a picturesque town with a historic fortress; Grinda, a beautiful island with sandy beaches and lush forests; and Sandhamn, a lively island with a rich maritime history. Prices vary depending on the duration and itinerary, but expect to pay around SEK 200-500 per person for a standard day trip.

8.2. Sigtuna - Sweden's Oldest Town

Founded in the late 10th century, Sigtuna is Sweden's oldest town and a treasure trove of history and culture. Located just a 45-minute drive or an hour's train ride from Stockholm, Sigtuna is an ideal destination for a day trip.

In Sigtuna, you can wander along the charming cobbled streets, lined with colorful wooden buildings, shops, and cafes. Be sure to visit the Sigtuna Museum (https://sigtunamuseum.se/en/), which offers fascinating insights into the town's history and the Viking Age. The museum is open daily, and admission is free.

Other attractions in Sigtuna include the picturesque St. Mary's Church, the ruins of St. Olof's and St. Peter's churches, and the Stora Gatan, the town's main street, which has been in use since the 10th century. Don't forget to explore the beautiful lakeside promenade and the Sigtuna Boardwalk, which offer stunning views of Lake Mälaren.

To reach Sigtuna by public transport, take the commuter train (pendeltåg) from Stockholm Central Station to Märsta, and then transfer to bus 570 or 575. The total journey takes approximately one hour, and a one-way ticket costs around SEK 90.

8.3. Uppsala - A Historic University City

Uppsala is a vibrant and historic university city located just 70 kilometers (43 miles) north of Stockholm. With a rich cultural heritage and bustling atmosphere, it makes for an excellent day trip destination.

The **Uppsala Cathedral,** Scandinavia's largest church, is a must-see. This stunning Gothic structure dates back to the 13th century and houses the relics of Saint Eric, the patron saint of Sweden. The cathedral is open daily and admission is free.

Uppsala University, founded in 1477, is the oldest university in Scandinavia. The university's main building, Universitetshuset, is an architectural gem with a beautiful courtyard. Don't miss the Gustavianum, the university's old main building, which now functions as a museum (https://www.gustavianum.uu.se/). Here, you can explore exhibits on archaeology, history, art, and science. Admission is SEK 70 for adults and SEK 40 for students and seniors.

The **Uppsala Castle** (http://www.uppsalaslott.se/) is another noteworthy attraction. The castle is home to the Uppsala Art Museum and offers panoramic views of the city from its hilltop location. Admission to the museum is SEK 50 for adults, while children under 18 enter for free.

To reach Uppsala from Stockholm, take the regional train (SJ) or the commuter train (pendeltåg) from Stockholm Central Station. The journey takes around 40-55 minutes, and a one-way ticket costs approximately SEK 100-200, depending on the train and booking method.

8.4. Drottningholm Palace and Gardens

Drottningholm Palace (https://www.kungligaslotten.se/english/royal-palaces-and-sites/drottningholm-palace.html) is the private residence of the Swedish royal family and a UNESCO World Heritage site. Located on the island of Lovön, just a 45-minute drive or boat ride from Stockholm, the palace and its beautiful gardens make for a delightful day trip.

The palace was built in the 17th century and is an outstanding example of a royal residence inspired by the Palace of Versailles. Visitors can explore the lavish state apartments, the exquisite palace theatre, and the palace church. Guided tours are available and included in the admission fee, which is SEK 140 for adults and SEK 70 for students. Children under 18 enter for free when accompanied by an adult.

The stunning palace gardens are a highlight of any visit to Drottningholm. The Baroque-style gardens feature perfectly manicured lawns, sculptures, fountains, and parterres, while the English park offers a more informal, natural landscape.

To reach Drottningholm Palace, you can take bus 176 or 177 from Brommaplan metro station, or enjoy a scenic boat trip with Stromma (https://www.stromma.com/en-se/stockholm/excursions/drottningholm/). The boat journey takes around one hour and costs approximately SEK 240 for a round-trip ticket.

8.5. Viking History and Cultural Experiences
Sweden has a rich Viking heritage, and the areas around Stockholm offer various opportunities to learn about and experience this fascinating period of history. Embark on a day trip to immerse yourself in Viking culture and discover the lives of these legendary seafarers, traders, and warriors.

- **Birka - The Viking City** (https://www.raa.se/birka/)
Birka, located on the island of Björkö in Lake Mälaren, is considered the most important Viking archaeological site in Sweden. As a former trading center and bustling port, Birka was at the heart of Viking life between the 8th and 10th centuries. Today, it is a UNESCO World Heritage site and an open-air museum where you can explore reconstructed Viking buildings, view archaeological finds, and attend guided tours. To reach Birka, take a boat tour from Stockholm with Stromma (https://www.stromma.com/en-se/stockholm/excursions/birka/). The round-trip ticket, including the guided tour, costs SEK 300-350 for adults and SEK 150-175 for children aged 6-15.

- **Sigtuna and The Viking Runestones**
As mentioned earlier in section 8.2, Sigtuna is Sweden's oldest town and boasts a rich Viking history. Alongside the town's other attractions, you'll find numerous runestones scattered throughout the area. These ancient stones, engraved with Viking inscriptions, offer a unique insight into the lives and beliefs of the Viking people.

- **Täby Kyrkby - Jarlabankes Bro**
Täby Kyrkby, located around 20 kilometers (12 miles) north of Stockholm, is home to Jarlabankes Bro, an impressive Viking bridge that is part of a larger ancient road system. The area also features a large concentration of runestones, providing a fascinating look into the region's Viking past. To get there, take the Roslagsbanan train from Stockholm Östra station towards Österskär and get off at Täby Kyrkby station.

- **Vikingaliv Museum** (https://www.vikingaliv.se/en/)
For those who prefer a more interactive and immersive experience, the Vikingaliv Museum in Stockholm's Djurgården district offers a journey through Viking history. This modern museum features exhibits, dioramas, and a thrilling ride called "Ragnfrid's Saga," which transports visitors back to the Viking Age. Admission is SEK 190 for adults, SEK 160 for seniors and students, and SEK 120 for children aged 7-15.

These day trips and experiences provide a fascinating glimpse into Sweden's Viking heritage, allowing visitors to better underst

9. Stockholm 3-Day Itinerary for First Timers

Day 1 Itinerary:
Skansen, Nordic Museum, Vasa Museum and Kaknästornet
Morning
Arrive in Stockholm and head to your hotel. Comprehensive information about getting into Stockholm city centre is provided earlier in this guide. Remember to pick up your Stockholm Pass from one of the collection desks if you need to.

11:00 am
First stop is the world's oldest open-air museum, Skansen. Here you can see how Swedes lived through the ages, take in the history and get to know some Nordic animals as well as some more exotic animals in the aquarium, which is home to Monkey World and over 200 exotic species. Additionally, Skansen is located on top of a hill and there are spectacular views of Stockholm from various different viewpoints. Skansen is very big and it's easy to spend the whole day enjoying every corner, however if you have limited time, there is a guide to visiting Skansen in 1 or 2 hours, highlighting the top sights. Skansen has various events throughout the year, so be sure to check out the goings on in the town square if you're visiting during a holiday period in particular. Depending on how hungry you are, you can grab a bite to eat from one of the stalls, or have something more substantial in one of the cafés or restaurants.

You can reach Skansen via the number 7 tram from Kunsträdgården. Admission costs up to SEK 195 depending on the time of year. Entrance to the aquarium is an additional SEK 120. Admission to both Skansen and the aquarium are included in the Stockholm Pass.

Part of the Sami settlement at Skansen

2:00 pm
After exploring everything Skansen has to offer, it's time to visit another of Stockholm's best tourist destinations, the Vasa Museum. Every Stockholmer you meet during your stay will ask you if you have been to this iconic museum, so pay attention! The Vasa is a warship that sunk in the Stockholm archipelago in 1628. It remained on the sea bed for 333 years before being salvaged and discovered to be in remarkably good condition. You can wander around this impressive ship in your own time, or alternatively there are guided tours in several languages.

To get to the Vasa Museum from Skansen you can either take the number 7 tram back towards the city, or alternatively it's only a short walk. Admission costs SEK 130 or is included in the Stockholm Pass.

The Vasa warship

3:30 pm
After the Vasa Museum you can pop next door to the Nordic Museum (Nordiska Museet). There are always many exhibitions at the Nordic Musesum, showcasing life in Sweden throughout history and up to the present day, including a wide range of aspects of Swedish life such as culture, lifestyle, art, interior design and traditions, so there is sure to be something you find interesting.

Admission to the Nordic Museum is SEK 120 (although it is free between 1:00 and 5:00 pm on Tuesdays) and is also included in the Stockholm Pass.

5:00 pm
When you have seen all you want to see at the Nordic Museum you can head towards Kaknästornet (tornet means tower in Swedish). This TV tower stands at 155-meters tall with excellent aerial views of Stockholm, making it

the perfect way to orientate yourself before you start to explore the city on day 2. Here you can enjoy dinner in the restaurant at the top of the tower, with 360 degree views of the city and the boats making their way out into the archipelago. It's best to book a table in advance to avoid the fee for going up in the lift. There is also an outdoor viewing platform at the very top of the tower if you want to feel the wind in your face. If you don't want to eat in the restaurant there is also a café and a bar on the floor above. For all your tourist souvenir needs, there is a gift shop on the ground floor.

It costs SEK 70 to go up the tower, but is free if you have a restaurant booking.

To get to the tower from the Nordic Museum you can take a lovely evening stroll, which takes about 35 minutes, walking along the water's edge and through the Nobel Park. Alternatively, if you don't want to walk, you can cross over the bridge by the Nordic Museum (Djurgårdsbron) and take the number 69 bus straight to Kaknästornet. The bus takes around 10 minutes.

Evening
If you want to go out in the evening you can either take the bus or walk back to Djurgårdsbron, from here it's just a short walk along the water before turning right at Dramaten theatre and heading up Birger Jarlsgatan towards Stureplan, which is popular for its classy nightlife. Stureplan is a small area, with several bars and restaurants all circling the centre, making it easy to find something to suit your taste. This is the place to go out if you want to dress up and enjoy the highlife, just be aware that, like many parts of Stockholm, it can be rather expensive.

Day 1 Map

Below you can get the map of all the suggested activities for your first day in Stockholm. This map is accessible in a Google Maps format so that you can quickly and easily view it on any device while on the go in Stockholm. Just click on the link below to access it.

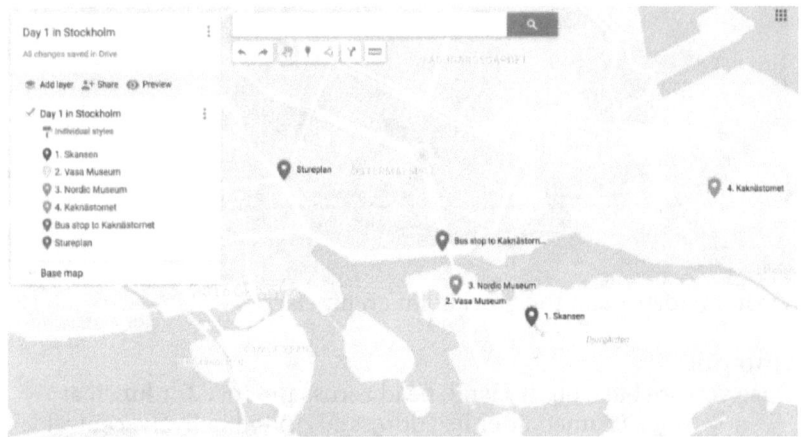

Get this map online in Google Maps format:
https://drive.google.com/open?id=1ohb8TfpGYGMSnnGr0x3MWLL9a6jNoZb8&usp=sharing

Day 2 Itinerary
Archipelago boat tour, Kungsträdgården, Royal Palace, Riddarholmen Church and Gamla Stan

10:30 am
After enjoying your hotel breakfast it's time to head to Strandvägen, berth 15/16 to join the archipelago boat tour. Stockholm's archipelago is tranquil and beautiful. It is one of the best features of the city, yet is often overlooked by people visiting for a short time. The tour offers you a peek into island life and the stunning scenery that every Stockholmer loves. You can book your ticket online in advance and then all you need to do is go directly to the boat and show the ticket as you board. If you have a Stockholm Pass, however, it is not possible to pre-book. In that case, you will need to go to the booking office on the day of the tour; it is worth bearing in mind that tickets are limited and so you should get to the ticket office early to avoid disappointment. More information regarding ticket pickup can be found on the Stockholm Pass website.

The tour takes between two and a half and three hours on a boat built in the early 1900s. You can sit inside or go out and enjoy the sea air up on the deck, just remember to wrap up warm in the winter months. There is a tour guide who offers interesting facts and history of the archipelago and there is also a café on board. If you want to save more time for exploring the city in the afternoon, you can book to have lunch during the tour.

The tour costs around SEK 295 per person or is included in the Stockholm Pass.

Vaxholm fortress in the Stockholm archipelago

1:00 pm
Once you are back on dry land, head across the road for lunch at Strandvägen 1 (named after its address). Located in lively, central Stockholm, it has a sophisticated-yet-relaxed vibe and is popular with locals and international travellers alike. After a relaxing lunch you can explore nearby Kungsträdgården (the King's garden), which is famed for its cherry blossoms in the spring and ice-skating rink in the winter. With its central stage, there are often events going on, so you never know what you might come across.

Fountain at Kungsträdgården

2:30 pm
From Kungsträdgården you can walk over the bridge Strömbron into the old town (Gamla Stan) and straight to the Royal Palace (Kungliga slottet), the official residence of the Swedish monarch. The Baroque-style palace is one of the largest palaces in Europe, with over 600 rooms spread across 11 floors. There are additionally several museums in the palace, including the Treasury, the Tre Kronor museum (detailing the palace's medieval history) and the armoury.

It costs SEK 160 per person to visit the Royal Palace, but admission is included with the Stockholm Pass. If you don't want to go in the palace, you can still walk around outside and get a good feel for the architecture.

The Royal Palace by night

4:00 pm
After exploring the palace you can take a five minute walk across Gamla Stan and to the small neighbouring island of Riddarholmen, home to Riddarholmen Church. Depending on the time of year (it is open in the summer and autumn) and how fast you get around the palace, you might have time to go into Riddarholmen Church, you can buy a joint ticket to go in the palace and the church, costing SEK 180. However, it is worth going just to have a look at the outside of the church which is steeped in history. It is Stockholm's only remaining medieval abbey and is the final resting place for Swedish royalty.

After exploring the church and Riddarholmen, you can make your way back to Gamla Stan and discover the streets of the oldest part of Stockholm. Dating back to 1252, Gamla Stan is one of the largest and most well-preserved medieval city centres in Europe and its narrow, cobbled streets make it a very charming destination. Be sure to keep a look out for the Iron Boy, the smallest statue in Stockholm, as well as Mårten Trotzigs Gränd, the narrowest alleyway in the city. It is also worth visiting the old town square, Stortorget, particularly in winter when there is a Christmas market.

The square (Stortorget) in Gamla Stan

Evening
Once you've exhausted yourself wandering the streets of Gamla Stan it's time to head to one of its many restaurants. Stockholms Gäsatbud, located at Österlånggatan 7 serves traditional Swedish food in a cosy, welcoming environment. For a more high-end dining experience, you can try Fem Små Hus, located on Nygränd 10. This Swedish-with-a-French-touch restaurant is located in the vaulted cellars of five houses (hence the name, which means "five small houses"), offering a very intimate dining experience.

After dinner, you can make your way towards the water and have a few drinks at Mr French, located on Tullhus 2. This is a popular spot, particularly in the summer, with its large outdoor area.

Day 2 Map
Below you can find the map with all the suggested places for your second day in Stockholm. You can click on the link to see it online in Google Maps making it easy to navigate your way round while in Stockholm.

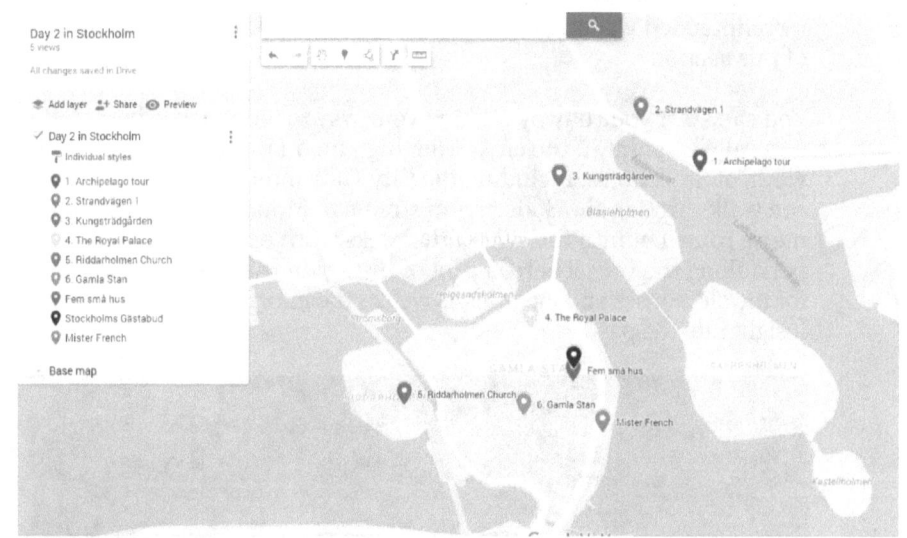

Click here to get this map online:
https://drive.google.com/open?id=1ImJzXLYiAdhtbIGo5JgWvB1QCCGUwZZQ&usp=sharing

**Day 3 Itinerary:
Södermalm and Fotografiska**

10:00 am
Day three is for exploring Södermalm, Stockholm's southern island, a recommended walking route is included in the online day 3 map at the end of this section.

You can start your day by making your way to Skinnarviksberget, the highest natural viewpoint in the city. From high up on this cliff you get panoramic views of Stockholm, including the City Hall and Gamla Stan. From here you can walk through the Södermalm streets to Monteliusvägen, a popular 500-metre route cut into the side of the rocks, with excellent viewpoints and a park along the way. There is a lot of history in this area, so keep an eye out for the old houses and factories as well as the information signs, giving a brief insight into the past.

A rare sighting of the northern lights from Monteliusvägen (photo by Micael Widell on Unsplash)

10:45 am
Once you reach the end of Monteliusvägen, take a walk through Mariatorget and on to Johan & Nyström, (Swedenborgsgatan 7) where you can have a coffee break. Coffee breaks, or "fika" in Swedish, are an essential part of Swedish culture and Johan & Nyström is known for some of the best coffee in town. To have a truly Swedish experience, make sure you get something

sweet to go with your coffee, if in doubt opt for a cinnamon bun, the most Swedish of all fika cakes. There is a more detailed guide to fika at the end of this book.

12:00 pm
After refuelling with fika, you can walk towards Hornsgatan, one of the main shopping streets in Södermalm and start walking towards the photography museum, Fotografiska. Along Hornsgatan you'll find a number of interesting shops, such as jewellery and design shops and small art galleries to browse in. Once you pass Slussen you get a great view across the water to the north of the city, including the rollercoasters of Gröna Lund. Before you head down the steps towards Fotografiska, which lies at the water's edge, it's worth taking a quick detour to Fjällgatan. Not only does this street offer yet more fantastic views of the city, but it is also home to wooden houses from the 1700s, giving you a real sense of what Stockholm would have been like hundreds of years ago.

View of the city from Fjällgatan (photo by Federico Enni on Unsplash)

1:00 pm
After your walk you will arrive at the photography museum. Fotografiska is popular with both locals and tourists, regularly holding new exhibitions by international and Swedish photographers. Aside from its excellent exhibitions, Fotografiska also has a superb restaurant and café with beautiful views overlooking the water. Here you can have a quick fika or take your time over a meal in the restaurant, which focuses on plant-based, ecological and seasonal food. On the weekends the restaurants holds a popular brunch

buffet, but you need to book several weeks in advance if you want to ensure you get a table.

Tickets to Fotografiska cost SEK 145 per person and are included in the Stockholm Pass. The brunch is SEK 395 per person and includes access to the exhibitions.

4:00 pm
After Fotografiska, it's time to head for an early dinner before beginning the journey back home. Just a 15-minute walk away from Fotografiska is the restaurant Kvarnen, situated in a traditional beer hall, it has been around since the start of the 1900s and has a cool, Södermalm vibe and serves great, traditional, Swedish food. A perfect way to round off your visit to Stockholm.

Day 3 Map
We have created an online Google Map with all the suggested places for your third day in Stockholm, including a recommended walking route to make sure you get all the best views. Click on the link below to view the recommended walking route.

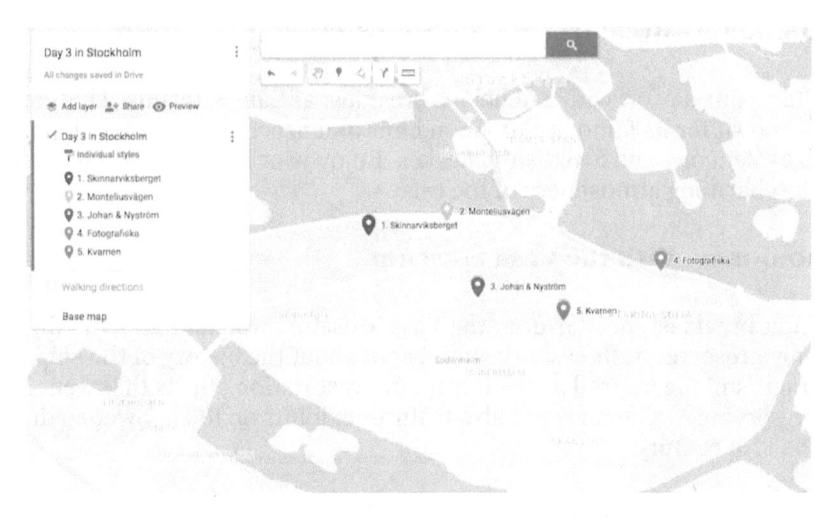

Click here to get this map online:
https://drive.google.com/open?id=14K4okdE2qgmiPNhQ14EVLs-l30nDjWjj&usp=sharing

10. Stockholm 3-Day Travel Itinerary for Couples

Day 1:

08:00am - Breakfast at Café Saturnus

Start your day off with a delicious breakfast at Café Saturnus. This cozy café is known for its famous cinnamon buns and hearty breakfast options, such as eggs Benedict and Swedish pancakes. Enjoy your breakfast while taking in the charming atmosphere of the café.

10:00am - Visit the Vasa Museum

After breakfast, head over to the Vasa Museum, which houses the world's only preserved 17th-century ship. Learn about the history of the ship and its tragic sinking, as well as the impressive restoration efforts that went into preserving it. The museum also features exhibits on life in Sweden during the 17th century.

12:00pm - Lunch at Östermalms Saluhall

After exploring the Vasa Museum, head to Östermalms Saluhall, a historic indoor food market that features a variety of food stalls and vendors. Grab lunch from one of the many vendors, such as the seafood-focused Lisa Elmqvist or the gourmet sandwich shop Gastrologik.

02:00pm - Walk through Gamla Stan

After lunch, take a leisurely stroll through Gamla Stan, Stockholm's charming Old Town. Explore the narrow cobblestone streets and colorful buildings, and visit some of the area's historic landmarks, such as the Royal Palace and Storkyrkan cathedral.

04:00pm - Visit Fotografiska

Next, head over to Fotografiska, a contemporary photography museum that features a variety of rotating exhibits from both established and up-and-coming photographers. The museum also has a restaurant and café with stunning views of the water.

07:00pm - Dinner at Oaxen

Slip End your first day in Stockholm with a romantic dinner at Oaxen Slip, a cozy waterfront restaurant that serves up modern Swedish cuisine with a focus on local and seasonal ingredients. Be sure to try the smoked Arctic char and the homemade sourdough bread.

Day 2:

08:00am - Breakfast at Greasy Spoon

Start your second day in Stockholm with breakfast at Greasy Spoon, a trendy café known for its delicious brunch options and cozy atmosphere. Try the pancakes with blueberry compote or the avocado toast with poached eggs.

10:00am - Visit the ABBA Museum

After breakfast, head to the ABBA Museum, which celebrates the iconic Swedish pop group. Explore interactive exhibits and displays featuring costumes, instruments, and other memorabilia, and even sing and dance along with virtual ABBA avatars.

12:00pm - Lunch at Urban Deli

After exploring the ABBA Museum, grab lunch at Urban Deli, a bustling market and café that features a variety of food stalls and vendors. Try the gourmet hot dogs or the fresh sushi rolls.

02:00pm - Explore Djurgården

After lunch, take a leisurely walk through Djurgården, a large park and recreational area that is home to a variety of museums, attractions, and outdoor activities. Visit the Skansen open-air museum, the Gröna Lund amusement park, or simply enjoy a scenic walk through the park.

06:00pm - Sunset boat tour

As the sun begins to set, take a romantic boat tour of Stockholm's archipelago, which consists of over 30,000 islands and islets. Many tour companies offer sunset tours that include dinner or drinks on board.

09:00pm - Dinner at Restaurang AG

End your second day in Stockholm with dinner at Restaurang AG, a trendy steakhouse that serves up high-quality meat dishes in a cozy and intimate atmosphere. Be sure to try the dry-aged ribeye or the Icelandic cod with brown butter.

Day 3:

08:00am - Breakfast at Café Pascal

Start your final day in Stockholm with breakfast at Café Pascal, a trendy café known for its artisanal coffee and delicious pastries. Try the homemade granola or the avocado toast with poached eggs.

10:00am - Visit the Royal Palace

After breakfast, head to the Royal Palace, the official residence of the Swedish monarch. Take a guided tour of the palace and explore the opulent rooms and halls, as well as the royal armory and treasury.

12:00pm - Lunch at Prinsen

After exploring the palace, head to Prinsen, a historic restaurant and bar that has been serving traditional Swedish cuisine since 1897. Try the classic Swedish meatballs or the smoked salmon.

02:00pm - Visit the Moderna Museet

After lunch, visit the Moderna Museet, a contemporary art museum that features a variety of works from both Swedish and international artists. Explore the museum's extensive collection, as well as its rotating exhibits **and installations.**

04:00pm - Explore the Stockholm City Hall

After the museum, take a walk to the Stockholm City Hall, a stunning building that is home to the city's government and is known for its impressive architecture and beautiful interior. Take a guided tour of the building and learn about its history and significance.

07:00pm - Dinner at Punk Royale

End your final day in Stockholm with a unique dining experience at Punk Royale, a modern restaurant that combines fine dining with a punk rock aesthetic. The multi-course menu changes frequently, but always features innovative and creative dishes.

The following table provides a list of all the places recommended in the three-day travel itinerary for couples to Stockholm. The table includes the name of the suggested spot, its website address, physical address, and GPS location. These details are useful for anyone who wants to easily find and navigate to each of the recommended places using Google Maps or other navigation apps.

Name of Suggested Spot	Website Address	Physical Address	GPS Location
Café Saturnus	https://www.cafesaturnus.se/	Eriksbergsgatan 6, 114 30 Stockholm	59.337931, 18.078940
Vasa Museum	https://www.vasamuseet.se/	Galärvarvsvägen 14, 115 21 Stockholm	59.328981, 18.091504
Östermalms Saluhall	https://ostermalmshallen.se/	Östermalmstorg 114 42 Stockholm	59.335394, 18.079717
Gamla Stan	https://www.visitstockholm.com/see--do/attractions/gamla-stan/	Gamla Stan, Stockholm	59.324895, 18.067033
Fotografiska	https://www.fotografiska.com/	Stadsgårdshamnen 22, 116 45 Stockholm	59.317174, 18.085372
Oaxen Slip	https://oaxen.com/slip/	Beckholmsbron 26, 115 21 Stockholm	59.319249, 18.103129
Greasy Spoon	http://www.greasyspoon.se/	Hagagatan 4, 113 48 Stockholm	59.342702, 18.055108
ABBA Museum	https://www.abbathemuseum.com/	Djurgårdsvägen 68, 115 21 Stockholm	59.324122, 18.096336
Urban Deli	https://www.urbandeli.org/	Nytorget 4, 116 40 Stockholm	59.314045, 18.085392
Djurgården	https://www.visitstockholm.com/see--do/attractions/djurgarden/	Djurgården, Stockholm	59.324023, 18.107384
Restaurang AG	https://restaurangag.se/	Kronobergsgatan 37, 112 33 Stockholm	59.334074, 18.047964
Café Pascal	https://www.cafepascal.se/	Norrtullsgatan 4, 113 29 Stockholm	59.347414, 18.049407
Royal Palace	https://www.kungligaslotten.se/english.html	Slottsbacken 1, 111 30 Stockholm	59.327389, 18.072500
Prinsen	https://www.prinsenrestaurang.se/	Mäster Samuelsgatan 4, 111 44 Stockholm	59.332499, 18.061468

Name of Suggested Spot	Website Address	Physical Address	GPS Location
Moderna Museet	https://www.modernamuseet.se/stockholm/en/	Exercisplan 4, 111 49 Stockholm	59.326270, 18.082307
Stockholm City Hall	https://international.stockholm.se/the-city-hall/about-the-city-hall/	Hantverkargatan 1, 111 52 Stockholm	59.327426, 18.054271
Punk Royale	https://punkroyale.se/	Mariatorget 1A, 118 48 Stockholm	59.317818, 18.065089

11. Stockholm 3-Day Itinerary For Families

Day 1:

08:00am - Breakfast at Café Schweizer

Start your day off with a delicious breakfast at Café Schweizer. This cozy café is known for its delicious pastries and traditional Swedish breakfast options, such as sandwiches and oatmeal.

10:00am - Visit Skansen

After breakfast, head over to Skansen, the world's first open-air museum. Explore the historic buildings and learn about traditional Swedish life and culture, as well as the many animals that call Skansen home. Don't miss the daily cultural performances, which include dancing, singing, and storytelling.

12:00pm - Lunch at Junibacken

After exploring Skansen, head to Junibacken, a children's museum and cultural center inspired by the works of beloved Swedish author Astrid Lindgren. Enjoy lunch at the museum's restaurant, which features a variety of kid-friendly options.

02:00pm - Visit the ABBA Museum

After lunch, head to the ABBA Museum, which celebrates the iconic Swedish pop group. Explore interactive exhibits and displays featuring costumes, instruments, and other memorabilia, and even sing and dance along with virtual ABBA avatars.

04:00pm - Visit Grona Lund

Next, head over to Grona Lund, Stockholm's historic amusement park. Enjoy the rides and attractions, as well as the many food and drink options. Don't miss the daily live performances by both Swedish and international artists.

07:00pm - Dinner at Meatballs for the People

End your first day in Stockholm with a family-friendly dinner at Meatballs for the People, a cozy restaurant that specializes in traditional Swedish meatballs made with locally sourced ingredients.

Day 2:

08:00am - Breakfast at Pom & Flora

Start your second day in Stockholm with breakfast at Pom & Flora, a trendy café known for its artisanal coffee and delicious pastries. Try the homemade granola or the avocado toast with poached eggs.

10:00am - Visit the Vasa Museum

After breakfast, head over to the Vasa Museum, which houses the world's only preserved 17th-century ship. Learn about the history of the ship and its tragic sinking, as well as the impressive restoration efforts that went into preserving it. The museum also features exhibits on life in Sweden during the 17th century.

12:00pm - Lunch at Östermalms Saluhall

After exploring the Vasa Museum, head to Östermalms Saluhall, a historic indoor food market that features a variety of food stalls and vendors. Grab lunch from one of the many vendors, such as the seafood-focused Lisa Elmqvist or the gourmet sandwich shop Gastrologik.

02:00pm - Visit the Moderna Museet

After lunch, visit the Moderna Museet, a contemporary art museum that features a variety of works from both Swedish and international artists. Explore the museum's extensive collection, as well as its rotating exhibits and installations.

04:00pm - Explore Djurgården

After the museum, take a leisurely walk through Djurgården, a large park and recreational area that is home to a variety of museums, attractions, and outdoor activities. Visit the Skansen open-air museum, the Gröna Lund amusement park, or simply enjoy a scenic walk through the park.

07:00pm - Dinner at Bakfickan